As Big as the Sky

A GEORDIE AT BAY

by

James Timmins

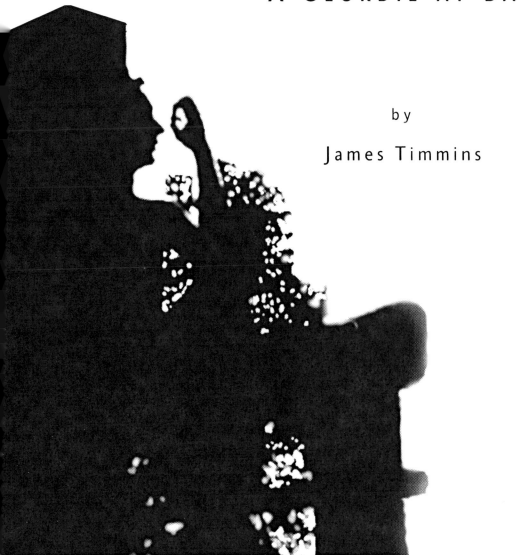

DEDICATION

This Final Story is for my children; Andrew, Julie, Sean, and my Grandchildren; Carrie, Daniel, Kanu, Molly, and Taylor.

I will always love you ... *"As Big As The Sky"*.

James Timmins, April 2006

"As Big As The Sky | A Geordie At Bay"

ISBN 978-1-4116-9687-7

Book Design and Layout by

KINGSWAY PRODUCTIONS TEL.408.881.2485

WWW.KINGSWAYPRODUCTIONS.COM

C O N T E N T S

* "Geordie" denotes a native of Newcastle-Upon-Tyne, England.

Canny folks they are, with a penchant for Travel and Adventure.

""Where ever ye gan, yel ' always find a **Geordie!***"*

A WARTIME CHILDHOOD

I was born on 29 September 1931 in Condercum road, Benwell Newcastle on Tyne, England. The Time: 5:15a.m. My brother Bobby and Sister Sheila were twins, born twenty months before. Mam said that the Doctor told her "the little girl is doing well, but I don't hold much hope for the boy" Well it so happens that Bobby grew up fine (and then some!), Did a stint in the British Army, got married and brought up a family. His Trade was that of Bricklayer, First Class, much in demand I might add. Well-done Bobby! Sheila did very well too; she has a son she is very proud of, and grandchildren to boot.

My Dad: Robert Joseph, came from Dublin, Ireland over to England when he was only 18 years old, I was told his brother Ned came too. Ned went to friends of his in Hull and Dad headed for Carlisle, where he took a job at the "County" Hotel as a Waiter. That is where he met my mother, her name: Lydia Trainer. They spent all their time off together and from what I gather Dad's Irish sense of humour had mam smiling as they tootled around Carlisle. After they had been courting for a while they came to Benwell, a suburb of Newcastle on Tyne where Mam's family lived. This City is situated twelve miles inland from the North East coast with the Scottish Border sixty miles to the North. It was here that they made plans to marry.

It may well be that the reader of this Tome is wondering why it is that I put pen to paper on the subject of "myself". Firstly this is a Family Document, not something to assuage the Ego. As I grew up, I have come to realize that my parents, bless them, did not think it important to tell their children very much about their childhood: anecdotes on brothers, sisters, how various ones met their spouses, even the background of their own parents. My intention is to leave this story for my Children and Grandchildren.

Marks Alley, Dublin

I have little knowledge of my Dad's side of the family, but I remember his Mam did correspond with him as we grew up, and on Saint Patrick's Day would send Shamrock for us kids to wear in our buttonholes. He spent his early years living on Marks Alley . . . within earshot of the bells of St. Patrick's Church! Truly, an Irishman! My son Andrew went to Dublin, visiting Dad's old haunts this past year, bringing it full circle. Almost all of my Mam's family lived in Newcastle; her parents lived in a small flat in Bond Street Benwell, (a suburb West of the city), as did Mam's sister Anna Belle. She married a Mr. Charles Wells, and they settled down in a flat (also in Bond street). In due course, they had two beautiful daughters, Joyce and Patricia, as well as a son;: Charles.

Joyce married an American soldier that she met during the Second World War and went to live in Maryland, USA. I was ten years old when my Mam took me to the local Parish church to see them married; I recall looking up at her from my seat during the ceremony and was surprised to see tears coursing down her face. Adults were still a mystery to me at that time. Now, about sixty years later, thanks to the magic of the Internet and Email, I've managed to contact Joyce and reminisce about the family.

After a few years, Joyce's younger sister Pat, wed a local man and lived in Benwell, Anna Belle's son Charles also married locally. Mam's Brother James, a bachelor for a long time, married and settled down outside Newcastle. Aunt Sarah lived with her husband Jack Black, in Canning Street, Benwell. Sister May and her husband Bill Henderson at the top of Larch Street also in that area, while her stepbrother Sam and his wife Ethel lived at the bottom of Westgate Road near the town centre. Sam served in the Army and was gassed in France which severely damaged his hearing, and left him unfit for regular work. However after much persistence he managed to get a post as dresser to the stars that came to perform at the Newcastle theatres.

Lastly, Sister Jesse married Bill Muttit, a Policeman and lived in South Shields, a town situated at the mouth of the river Tyne. Two daughters were born to them, Jesse and Iris, eventually both of the girls' married Canadian service men. Jesse and Iris of course were my cousins. But I digress, Mam and Dad, got married and their first home was a Flat in Ravensworth Terrace just behind Westgate road near the downtown area. As a matter of interest, the street sign "Ravensworth Terrace" now graces the main street at the open air Museum at "Beamish" not far from Newcastle. Soon a little girl was born to them, "Mary", but she died after only a few months, then of course, the Twins, Bobby and Sheila arrived.

Around this time, Dad took a position as a Waiter with the Railway, and later at the Turks Head Hotel in Grey Street, Newcastle. The larger family made it necessary to seek another place to live, and so it was that they moved to Condercum Road, Benwell, whereupon I arrived upon the world stage. Sister Margaret would be born 8 years later in Pendower.

In the period of 1933 to 1935, I have recollections of me playing on the sidewalk outside our house and in the back lane with my friends, I had a small red pedal car and my brother Bobby had a tricycle, I remember, even at that age feeling slightly superior, being "the one with the car". Our house was of the "Terrace" type on the street level, containing two Bedrooms, a Living Room (although it was always called "the Kitchen") and a "Scullery" where the cooking and clothes washing were done. (Don't ask) The laundry was done in a gas-heated copper tub that was open at the top. Mam would stand there, agitating the clothes by vigorous use of a "Poss Stick". This was a copper suction device on the end of a wooden shank. Woe Betide any delicate fabrics that found their way into the dreaded "Poss Tub".

We also had a back yard with a "Coal House" which was simply a brick built storage shed adjacent to the "outside toilet". Mam told me many years later that she once found me in the Back Yard, having "captured" all the neighbours cats from the lane at the back of the house, Maybe this was a reprisal on my part for her "getting rid" of "Bobby's cat" while we kids were at the "pictures" one Saturday morning. Being fair though, Mam did try to make amends by buying a soft toy cat for him, the Story goes that Bobby, crying, grabbed it, flung it across the room, and then shouted "you not a *real* pussy cat!"

8

In the living room (Kitchen) there was an open range fireplace, which heated an oven situated at one side, on the wall above was a "mantle shelf" which held some ornaments and a few Knick-Knacks. Having little ones in the house made it necessary, even imperative to have a Fire guard in front of the Fireplace, the one we owned was constructed of steel wire mesh with a beveled brass rail running along the top. In front of it stood a Fender with a fender box seat at each end of the Fireplace, the name: Fender came from the job it did of stopping hot cinders from falling from the fire and rolling onto the floor.

It was Christmas time 1934 when I was three years old, Bobby and I were tucked up in bed in the front bedroom, (I guess, so that Mam could get on with "Christmas things"). Bobby was being very "naughty" yelling about how there really no one was going to deliver free toys to our house. Just about then, my uncle Bill paid a visit. He was on his way to a County police function with the Chief of Police and was calling to wish us all a merry Xmas. I recall how smart he looked in his uniform.

Now, Uncle Bill although a Policeman in South Shields, was also an accomplished conjurer (known as Ali Ben Mutt) working in Northeastern theatres, I would add that he was also a damn good Ventriloquist. He came into our bedroom and Bobby proceeded to tell him "how it really was." Uncle Bill walked over to the small fireplace there and he called up the chimney to Santa Claus, Lo and Behold a gruff old voice came back *"I won't come down there while they're awake"!* --Voila two little boys fast asleep.

I wish today that I'd been able to get to know Uncle Billy a little more, but we only got to visit South Shields about once a year or so. Their home was in the Police building in the centre of town, and many's the time that he had us kids wide eyed showing us his skills with sleight of hand tricks. At some point in the day he would take us down to the yard to see the fire engines, we were allowed to climb on them, sit in the driver's seat, and even ring the bell. It was at these times that I just knew I would be a Fireman one day. Uncle Billy passed away in recent years, but on my last visit to see him, he told me how he was developing some "tricks" for his friend the popular Conjurer Tommy Cooper, a World famous TV Star. I was to learn later in life that he was awarded Medals for bravery in the First World War; one of them was for saving the life of a fellow soldier. The nightmare of the war left him reluctant to speak of it to anyone.

Again, I digress, so back we go to our front room in Condercum road Benwell. It was in this same room at a later date that I was chastised for spinning around with arms outstretched and was told that I might even fall into the fireplace, and guess what, one day...I did, but fortunately it was summertime and there was no fire lit, which was just as well as I landed on it seat first. Now it so happened that all afternoon Mam and Dad had been "having words," Dad was in the room as I fell onto the Grate and he was sitting by the window somewhat tipsy. I cried out in Pain and yelled to him for help, but he just replied, "call your Mother", Wow Dad! You sure must have been upset with Mam.

In the back lane, at the rear of our house in Benwell were some Businesses; Workshops, Storage Sheds, and the like. Behind them on some spare ground was a Blacksmiths Shop. We kids would stand at the door looking in wonder at the Blacksmith, sweat running off him, pumping the bellows and holding up the hoof of what appeared to me to be a huge horse, then applying the hot shoe and nailing it on. The horse itself showed no sign of any discomfort, but even today, I find it a source of puzzlement.

Newcastle Upon Tyne

Neville Street

Grainger Street

Northumberland Street

Stretching beyond the blacksmiths shop to the West as far as the "New Pendower Estate" were some allotments and spare ground. For some reason we called it "The Quarry". It was a wonderful playground I myself would become transformed into a Cowboy I'd seen in a film, Buck Jones, perhaps or Tom Mix as I galloped across the Prairie shooting down all the bad guys I could conjure up. As my fancy would take me I would be a brave Policeman and using the burned out shell of an old car just behind the blacksmiths shop, I would careen madly after the gangsters.

Right opposite our front door was the "Majestic Picture House", the source of my imaginings, and on Saturday Mornings Brother Bobby, Sheila and I would go to the Matinee show, the cost of a ticket ...Tuppence! It surely was a bargain: a cartoon a serial, "Flash Gordon" perhaps or the "Clutching Hand" and the main feature Wow! One thing I would like to mention here is that whenever the bad guy would begin to creep up behind the Hero or the heroine, the whole audience of kids would erupt in cries of "Nit"! This signaled a warning. To this day, I do not know the origin of this splendid word.

Condercum Road, Benwell

The Grand Cinema Palace   *The Majestic*

Of course, let us not forget the "*Grand Cinema Palace*". This theatre, (it was opposite the *Majestic* and a few yards down the street) at the corner of Elswick Road, it was much smaller in seating capacity than the Majestic and a little older but it put on some good pictures. Every so often, a live Stage show would be presented and very popular they were too. Sitting at the intersection of our street and Elswick Road, she did well from walk-in traffic, but as luck would have it, the Stalls (cheaper seating), attracted a large number of "rowdies", who spoiled it for everyone else. This also hurt the Cinema's reputation.

When I was about seven years old, Bobby and myself became friendly with the lady who sold tickets for the rear stalls. (Very Posh) and on Friday nights she'd have us go to the Fish Shop in Bond Street to buy A "Fish and sixpen'orth" for her supper and in exchange we'd get a free seat to see a movie "very acceptable!" (I sometimes wonder if she noticed that she was a few chips short). A memory, which is indelibly in my mind regarding the Theatre itself, is an audible one. When living in Pendower, I was at times sent on errands, which took me past the "Grand", and this sound could be heard, even from a distance, for hours on end whenever the building was in use. It was the noise made by the exhaust from the generator room, which was carried up to the roof through a six-inch pipe stack, a sort of Thunk, Thunk, Thunk sound. Who knows, maybe it was just the "Cinema" (as we knew it) trying to be heard above the noise. The years went by and as luck would have it, the "Grand Cinema Palace" became known as the "Loppy Opera", the "Flea Pit" and then affectionately as the Ranch, pity, because she always delivered the goods.

When I was four years old my family moved from Benwell to Riddle Avenue, Pendower Estate and into a Council House, My Dad had a friend, named "Walter" who also lived in Condercum Road, he owned a "lorry" and helped us to "shift". ("Note the vernacular, I think it belongs) Three bed rooms and, of all things, a toilet inside the house. These homes had gaslight installed for illumination; I can only surmise that the "powers that be" at that time were not yet convinced that "Electricity was here to stay". (Although the house was wired later).

The gas supply was terminated at a mantle suspended from the ceiling in the middle of the room, and was lit of course by striking a match, it was nothing short of a miracle that there were not more fires and explosions in the area. The mantle was fed via a Gas meter sitting on a shelf in the scullery; it also supplied gas to the gas oven in the scullery. This meter demanded pennies in order that we could sit in the evening and have some light, or have a kettle heated to make tea. (As I recall there were a few pennies kept at one end of the mantle shelf within easy reach). We will not talk about the times a meal was spoiled when the gas was cut off and we perhaps had no change. Being fair though a "Shilling meter" was installed after a few years.

There came a time when Bobby and I were sleeping in the room situated above the scullery and it was there that we had a narrow escape. Bobby woke up and smelling gas he got out of bed and sleepily opened the window wide, and was about to go back to bed, when the situation dawned on him, and he yelled at me to get up. We then ran to wake up Mam and dad. Using a wet cloth over his nose and mouth dad entered the scullery, found the oven key in the "on" position and turned it off. Sadly, the family cat was found dead with her three kittens in the act of clawing at the back door. It was decided that as dad reached up to put money into the meter before going to bed, his pants pocket must have caught on the gas key turning it on.

The kitchen there was the same kind of open fireplace with an oven that we had been used to in Benwell. This one also heated a hot water tank at the rear. Oh, joy! Hot baths on demand? Not quite, a roaring fire would usually supply about two inches of hot water in the bath, but we muddled along, grateful for even that. The "Scullery" contained yet another gas heated Poss tub of course, but best of all, this house was semi detached with a garden front and back. We were to live in this house for about 20 years and I have many happy memories of our life there. By way of confession, when we moved in on the first day I had a great time running up and down stairs and all over the house, but as twilight settled in I requested that as I was tired, I wanted to "go home". From what I understand, Mam and Dad had to do some fancy talking to convince me that "this *was* home".

At Four years old I began my attendance at a pre-school named Ashfield Nursery School, Taken as I was by tramcar about two miles along Elswick Road I was left to learn how to socialize, play games, listen to stories and generally enjoy myself. I'm surprised that I can remember these things from such an early age, I even recall that the lady in the kitchen had a Parrot and that we little ones were allowed at times, to visit and listen to him talking. The other gem is the times that our teacher would have us walk in twos holding hands down an external steel fire escape to reach the garden at the back of the building. She called it "the Fairy stairs" so we must go down on our tip toes holding hands and "no talking", all this so as not to disturb the children on the lower floors

Many good times were to be had in our street summer or winter. Kids about my age were John, Audrey, Iris, Dorothy, my sister Sheila and brother Bobby of course. Other boys in our street were very old I am afraid, twelve or so at least, their names were Peter, Neil and Gordon. The games we played were many and varied, "Tally-ho," "Up for Monday" "Halibilevo", even a game called "Tuggy little man."

Seasons brought games of tops and whips, Kite flying etc. Girls it seems were forever skipping or putting on shows in Shirley Temple style while we boys' favoured games of "Jumbo" or "Soccer", our jackets thrown on the ground marked the "goal posts" (poor Mam).

There was also the game of "Pirates". Using the sidewalk as a "ship", the older boys made us young' ns as members of the crew, "walk the plank" represented by the "Black line", a twelve inch wide section of road which at some time had been excavated to facilitate repairs to a drain, then patched and now could be seen quite clearly.

At other times we would have a pursuit game on the two sidewalks and the only places one could cross between the two was at either of the two lamp posts in the street. It should, I think be mentioned here that in order to be excused from capture in any of the games mentioned, one only had to yell the password "skinchys!, what a strange word, and I don't even know if I've spelled it correctly.

One morning whilst playing in the street I was told by a breathless friend that there was a fire in Benwell at a factory that produced Wafers of various shapes and sizes used by Ice Cream vendors. A couple of friends and myself raced off at top speed to watch the Fire Brigade at work. The unfortunate establishment was just behind Larch Street and as we arrived it could be seen that the whole building was fully involved. Pushing my way to the front, I stood and for the first time I felt the horror of the fire as it literally consumed the building in what seemed a cauldron of malicious smoke and flame. Soon we noticed that large boxes of wafers had been salvaged and were standing to one side, imagine our delight as we were told that we could take away as much as we could carry. An afternoon feast was soon in progress at our favourite "Smeck" on the Quarry, I guess our parents wondered why we were off our food that night.

In those days, the area was serviced by Tradesmen with Horse Drawn Carts, or in the case of the COOP Milk, a Lorry (a commercial Truck, the precursor of things to come). A mobile Greengrocer, Fishmonger, the Ringtons Tea man, and of course the Ragman, rounded out the mix, The Ragman would blow a cacophony of notes on a battered old Trumpet to announce his arrival. He offered Balloons or a Gold fish for old clothes or bottles etc; He was a great favourite with all the neighborhood children, who would dash off madly to ask their folks for the wherewithal. One day my Mam returned from shopping only to find that some clothes items (I know not what) had gone from a drawer. It sure was a mystery, and we three kids were the only ones at home. Oh Well! The only sound that could be heard was the Rasping voice in the next street shouting "Any Rags . . . Bottles . . . or Jam Jars, accompanied of course by the bizarre call of his trumpet.

I began my formal education when I was five years old at Canning Street School in Benwell, crossing the quarry to get there, which was great fun rain or shine. It was on one of my trips to school across the quarry that I found a big heap of dummy (display) chocolate bars dumped there and promptly stuffed my pockets with a large selection of them. On reaching school, I gave them out to friends who eagerly accepted them, but their joy turned to dismay when they saw that they were not real, so I was obliged to make myself scarce for a while. It was an older School with a reputation for discipline but we kids did not mind too much, besides it boasted a simply huge play yard and we made full use of it even though it had a hard surface.

A favourite game of ours when in the school yard was "Stage Coaches", it involved running with a friend, hands clasped behind our backs, one day I tripped and fell face first onto the ground, this made a real mess of my nose and mouth I cried out in pain as blood spurted everywhere. As I lurched towards the school door to get some help a friend of mine; Andy, kept the crowds back that were surging around me, arms outstretched shouting, "keep back! We might get blood poisoning"! (It is entirely possible that Andy is a renowned Surgeon somewhere today). I was cleaned up and sent home and Mam put me to bed with a hot water bottle, She then went to the stores at the foot of Pendower way (known to us kids as the bottom shops) and returned with a comic for me, next, as I remember she made tea, boiled egg, toast, Lovely.

The only Shopping centre of any consequence within walking distance was in Benwell. It was a section of Elswick Road called "Adelaide Terrace" stretching roughly from "Atkinson road" to "St. Johns Road". Most anything could be bought there, from groceries to shoe repairs, from Pharmaceuticals to second hand clothes, even fish and chips.   This proved to be a boon to the local folks as it meant that a trip to most stores only took a few minutes and there were no Bus fares involved besides it was a great place to meet friends and catch up with some gossip.

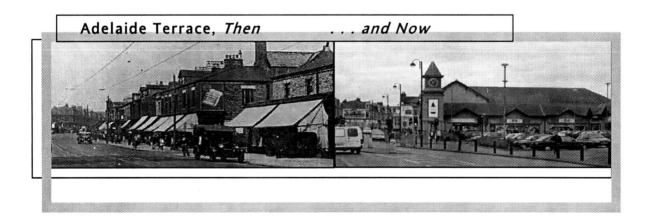

Adelaide Terrace, *Then*   *. . . and Now*

At Xmas time we kids would at times head for "Story's" Ironmongers Shop at the intersection of Adelaide Terrace and Clara Street. We would stand transfixed at a window that Mister Story had dressed for the season. It was snowing at times and we would stamp our feet and blow on our frozen fingers to keep circulation going, but we would not move from this magic scene in the window, greedily drinking it in as if there was no tomorrow. Coloured lights lit up the scene. A model railroad: Mountains, lakes, a town with tiny cars and people, and various trains stopping and starting at their appointed places.

I remember Mr. Story very well, as he moved about his Store, he wore a cap and an old Jacket worn over his oil stained overalls. There was always a lick of his hair hanging over one eye, his hands, toil worn from handling creosote, Paraffin, small bundles of firewood and hundreds of other items the smell of which assailed ones nostrils upon entering the establishment as he busily helped his customers. I do not suppose for a moment that he realized the Joy he brought to at least one little urchin standing in the snow outside his window.

My Dad was a great Storyteller; we three kids would sit around the fire in the evening clutching the brass rail of the Fireguard staring into the dancing flames wearing our pajamas. Dad's Irish voice (I can hear it now) conjuring up the wicked witch as she plotted against the three Piggies that lived in the woods (The Piggies always came out best of course) Usually the Witch met a bizarre end, as Dad often had her turned into a pillar of salt. What an imagination! He sure could tell 'em.

On a Friday (Payday) Dad, on his way from work, would at times bring home some goodies, a few slices of chicken or turkey, courtesy of his good friend the Chef at the Turks Head Hotel. At other times he would buy fish and chips for us all and perhaps a Baby Guinness for Mam, this last item was a wise choice as he had at times had a couple of pints himself on the way home. Friday was a good day for us kids too because Dad gave us our pocket money, three pence each, we'd race off to the bottom shops to buy a comic each and some sweets at the News agents. Mam and Dad would sit having supper at the kitchen table and talking while we kids had a small table by the fire, a few chips and our comics: Ah Bliss!

16

Mam and Dad could never afford Holidays as such, but I recall with much happiness that, if the weather were nice we kids would be taken for the day to Whitley Bay, (a coastal resort town about twelve miles away). The weather was always of concern to Mam and dad at this time. When the sky seemed to cloud over Mam would make comments about possible rain and even remove her hat, sit down, make tea etc, all the while we kids prayed to Heaven that the sun would make an appearance, actually, we were always lucky as I don't recall ever being disappointed on this score. Mam would pack some sandwiches and a flask of tea, put it in her shopping bag then off we would go. The Tramcar could not go fast enough for me as we headed towards the city centre, magic was literally in the air. We three kids chattered away all the time while pointing out things we knew as we passed them, the Adelaide Picture Hall, the Elswick coal Company, (our supplier) Ashfield nursery school, the "Big Lamp" and lastly a wind direction indicator on Westgate Road known to we three little ones as the "Windmill." Once off the tram we would walk to the Central station in Neville Street, on the way Mam would, on occasion, have us stop by "Jerome's", a photography Studio to have a family picture taken. Of course we would have preferred to get to the Station instead we were so excited, (After all the last train may have left!)

Dad, having worked as a Waiter on the railway, had friends in the station, and I would hear him greet some of them as we walked through the station, Mam might ask "who was that?" and Dad's reply was always be the same, "One of our Fellas." Being a nice day of course there'd be a big line up for the Electric Trains and when we reached the front Dad ushered his three kids through, (I can feel his hand on my shoulder right now) as he gave the Porter a big smile a sly wink and handed him *two* tickets.

We settled down in the train and waited, meanwhile I have, more than once, spotted a huge steam train thundering through the station and asked, "Which train is that Dad?" "Oh that's the London to Glasgow Express," he might say, I was in awe of him and his knowledge. He might have been just guessing of course, but it is a Dad's privilege to tell a fib or two in a case like this.

We all enjoyed the train journey as you might expect and hurried out of the station then on down Station road. Parents and children galore, all eager to get to the beach, I was terribly afraid that someone might get there before us. It was about a quarter of a mile or so to the sea and the street was lined with shops that sold all of the paraphernalia needed for the beach and more besides. As we walked along clutching our spades and pails, we kids could see that there were people at tables in the windows of quite posh Cafes enjoying a meal, but not once did I wonder why it was that *we* did not go in to eat; it seemed enough to me just to be there. Between you, me and the gate post, I wondered why on earth adults were wasting time in there when they could be on the beach, however, grown up people did behave strangely at times and no error.

On the beach we played the usual kids games, Mam and Dad sat and talked or dozed, Dad has been known to take off his shoes and socks, roll up his pants six inches or so and take us for a "plodge" in the sea.   Building sand castles took up much of the time, as I remember. I cannot help but feel the harshness of the sand in between my toes as I write. The highlight of the day for me was the Donkey Rides, an Attraction found at most of Britain's beaches. Consisting of a dozen or so animals strung together, their owners would lead them on a circuit of their choosing through the sand. They were quite docile and children would line up, hand over a copper or two, be hoisted up into the saddle and off we would go. It was spell binding for me as once again I was transformed into a cowboy rounding up cattle as I had seen many times in films. I was at last brought out of my reverie with a jolt as the jingling of harnesses ceased and I was placed back on Terra Firma.

In need of refreshment we would be taken along the lower Promenade to a small Cafe, not much of a place, bare floor, bare tables, very austere, their total menu consisted of sandwiches, small cakes, and tea. Once inside, we would sit down and Mam would order Tea, she would then pass us a sandwich under the table from her shopping bag, a notice on the wall told us "Customers must not bring in their own food," such were the times we lived in. As the day wore on we, at times, would watch the Punch and Judy Show on a section of grass on the sea front reserved for this time honoured Show, we children would hunker down on the grass and yell warnings to the characters on stage where needed, and a good time was had by all. Later we were taken to the Spanish City Amusement Park, Mam liked the " Roll your Penny" stalls (Joel's Rolls) whilst we kids favoured the "Rides" especially the "Paddle Boats", Dad would just watch out for us and very soon would make sure that we would get to sample the local Ice cream. Lovely!

Often, Mam and Dad would take a walk on the "Links" which was a grassy area filled with banks of flowers and such overlooking the sea, we children of course ran around playing Hide and Seek etc. and generally wore our selves out. Evening came, and sometimes Dad would take Mam to a sea front Pub and while we children sat on a bench outside munching Smiths Crisps and Drinking "Tizer", they would spend a little time inside on their own.

Later perhaps, walking along the sea front we would see the Beam of Saint Mary's Lighthouse shining out to sea and the twinkling lights of ships as they `plied their trade to and from the River Tyne.  All too soon, it was time to go home, and we walked towards` the train station. Bobby, Sheila and I subdued by now, walking in front and quite hungry, but wait! Here's a Fish and Chip shop, Mam and Dad would take us in, Result? Three contented children. I was quite often asleep on Dad's knee as the train moved off to Newcastle, and thence onto the Tram which took us back to Pendower meanwhile Mam would tell every one that cared to listen: "Jimmy's the baby of the family, He'd sleep on a clothes line". I'd wake up in bed the next day thinking of the great day we'd had.

Mind you, a trip such as this was not always fun. There was the time during the War when Aunt Sarah and Mam brought us kids on a trip to Whitley Bay along with Sister Margaret who was about two years old at the time. All the amusements were closed; ominous signs on the lower promenade told us that mines were deployed on the sands that we loved so well therefore we did the next best thing, sitting there all afternoon on the prom gazing out to sea. Barbed wire was strung out along the sea front that served to keep folks off the beach as well as the German Army away from us (we would have destroyed them). But the weather was good so we walked a lot.

It was whilst walking on the Links that Mam noticed that Margaret was no longer with us. After initial panic and running around the flower beds it was agreed that she must have wandered further afield so Mam called the police station and a search was organized. We had no luck on the sea front and although we could not imagine a little tot finding her way safely across the main North/South Coast road, (we were to find later that this is exactly what she had done). So Mam, very frightened by now, walked up Marine Avenue with a Police official, searching all the while. Imagine Mam's surprise and delight when she espied an old lady sitting outside her front door, with little Margaret who was enjoying a glass of milk and some biscuits. Mam was told that my young sister had simply walked up to her front door explaining that she was hungry. Quickly, the lady sent a message to the Police Station, then went indoors and produced the snack for her. Just then, Mam arrived. All of our party gathered around the happy wanderer . . much hugging and kissing and of course, many thanks to the kind lady. We were then all taken inside her cottage for a nice cup of tea and a discussion about the Incident.

The other big treat for Newcastle children was in June in what was known as "Race week," That's when the "Hoppins" take place, better known as a fairground; it is purportedly the largest one of its kind in Great Britain. Stretching almost the full length of the Town Moor, (a huge stretch of grassland owned by the City) it brought Showmen from the length and breadth of Britain. Everything was there, from Freak Shows to the Helter Skelter from Dodge'Em Cars to Bingo, Coconut Shies to Peep Shows. Burned into my memory is the lady who called out to the passing crowds while standing outside a marquee filled we were told with "lovely ladies" "If you're shy close one eye, but have a jolly good look through the other one." Some of them she said came all the way from a harem in faraway Egypt. It must have been true because I saw them on the bus going home to Benwell after work clutching their fish and chips supper wrapped in a copy of the Sunday Sun.

Special Bus Services were laid on from all over Newcastle area, Mam and Dad took us most every year on a Bus that left from the top of Hodgkin Park road and went along Elswick road then up Bentinck road, along Hunters road as far as Claremont road, we'd then walk across the Moor to the "Hoppins". To spend all day there was enough to make a little Lads head spin and it was three tired children that climbed wearily back onto the bus for the return trip. A quick cup of Cocoa and then off to bed, perchance to dream! Mind you, sometimes we three kids would have a pillow fight in bed perhaps just to finish off a wonderful day, but for some strange reason we found that Mam and Dad felt the ensuing noise too much to bear. Dad would call out to us with dire threats, but when he and mam finally came up the stairs to our room, we were always magically fast asleep. In my minds eye I can see them smile at each other as they left the room and quietly closed the door.

The Pendower association was quite involved with putting on special events for the children living on the estate, Christmas parties at the Pendower hall, etc. In the summer time, before the war a couple of shiny red single deck buses would be parked on Pendower Way on occasion as part of the day trips for children program. Soon both conveyances were chock full of children shrieking and laughing, and wanting to know why it was that we were not speeding down the Kings highway. Soon of course, we were, and the driver was obliged to sit there listening to the melodious voices of the boys and girls behind him as we sang (yelled) such songs as "Oh the drivers got the wind up" (but I'm sure he brought his own Aspirins,) all the way to Tynemouth or maybe Cullercoats. It surely must have been a hair raising sight for the locals to see so many laughing, chattering children pouring out of the buses, and streaming onto the beach clutching spades, pails and sandwiches (not a parent in sight) only a couple of volunteers from back home. A good time was had by all of course, the day flew by and all too soon we were called to board our buses. Bedraggled, bruised and shoes full of sand we headed for home. I am sure the reader can picture the scene as we retraced our journey to canny Newcastle in the darkness, no voices raised, most of us asleep, and the engine a steady roar in the night.

Sheila was special to me, after all not many other boys had an older Sister, she would always be there to hear about my little problems and help where she could. Always the young lady, she was the nightingale of the family and sang most all the time she was at home, somewhat on the lines of "Kathryn Grayson" an American Movie star of that period. Sometimes a relative would come to visit and hope to hear her sing, but Sheila was very shy and as I recall, never did oblige. Pity! The only time I recall Sheila getting into trouble was when she was about ten years old or so, she went with Bobby to the Hoppins and they foolishly spent all of the money they had, including their return bus fare. The result was that they were obliged to walk home. Mam and Dad were upset, naturally, and of course they duly read them the riot act. Bobby proved to be the adventurous one. I believe he fell *off*, *onto*, or *into* most everything. He was knocked down by vehicles quite a few times and seemed to always have scraped knuckles from practicing the art of fisticuffs. Strange thing was, he was not a big person, and I think he was just trying to prove that Doctor wrong. One of the many road accidents which occurred at the foot of Pendower Way knocked Bobby clean out, and he was duly rushed to Hospital. Where I am told he recovered after being unconscious for a few days I recall Mam got a letter from the Matron a few days later begging her to come at once to take her little boy home. It appears that Bobby was causing chaos in the ward, pestering other patients and nurses, and could generally be seen clambering around everywhere.

On Saturdays in the Summer there were many Weddings at our local Church, St. James's on Elswick Road, and an old custom allowed us lads to get a little extra "loot". It was the practice called "Hoy Oot" (translated: "throw out"). The Wedding Party was expected to throw a little money out of the car window for the local urchins before driving off, by way of encouragement we would chant in the local jargon, "Hoy oot" (just in case they were somewhat shy). Moreover, if they were not forthcoming we would shout after the car such endearments as "Yah, Rotten Wedding"! (Charming little boys). With luck we'd see a shower of coins thrown onto the road, followed I might add by a scene of Mayhem as the Lads went in the same general direction as the money, elbows flying, grabbing for coins. I forgot to mention that this was a main thoroughfare and many was the times we'd hear the clanging of a tram drivers Bell as he, using colourful language I might add, sought to proceed on his lawful way. However, being that age we all thought him a miserable old spoilsport after all the stakes were high for us.

Quite often there'd be more than one Wedding that day, and I could be seen after a while trudging   home   clutching   some pennies, and if I was lucky perhaps a thrupenny bit or two, even, "Please Lord" a sixpence (known in the vernacular as a "Tanner"). The other custom at the Church would be when a child was christened; the parents would have with them a small package containing sweetmeats. On leaving the Church they would invariably run into at least one of us boys "strolling by", the package would be presented to the first child they met, who was the same sex as their Baby, all this to bequeath Good Luck on the child, very tasty, and of course I always prayed for little boys.

Being a working class area, there were Pawnshops in Benwell. It was not unknown for Mam to wrap Dad's only suit in brown paper, hand it to me or Bobby to take there, and to request a couple of shillings. This would only happen in times of sheer desperation of course, and Mam would instruct that, should we meet with anyone and be asked "What's in the parcel?" I was to say "I'm taking Dad's suit to the cleaners"; looking back I realize that the trick was "to Survive". It's strange but as I read what I've written about us, it seems to describe an impoverished family. This was not quite true, but we had to cut corners, *make do* where we could, and *do without* where we had to. A case in point: Dad had a friend who was a Barber with a shop on Adelaide Terrace, his name was Fraser and there were times that Dad would tell me to "go and get a haircut" and tell Mr. Fraser that "your Dad would give him the money at the weekend." I do so hope that he did not forget. Just another sign of the times I guess.

In 1937-1938 Mam took a job in the Admiralty Ordnance Bond at the factory on Scotswood Road and we had a baby sitter for a while, a nice lady Mrs. McCabe was her name, she lived in Benwell and would come to our house to keep an eye on us during the day while Mam was at work. Although there were three of us to care for I do not think, we gave her much anxiety. Mind you there was the time that Bobby took a box of matches into the small bathroom and set fire to the paint on the wall with the aid of some newspaper, our babysitter dashed in and threw a jug of water over it and extinguished it. I think she threw the empty vessel at Bobby, but I'm not sure. She would, at times take us to *her* house for the day where we'd explore every nook and cranny and generally leave the house in disarray. If the weather was nice she might take us on the Tramcar to Elswick Park to let off some steam, roll on the grass and have a go on the swings, or as she herself would put it "Have a Hycky." If time permitted on a particular day, she would choose "Leazes Park" instead, near the centre of town. This was a bigger Park with a lake and an even bigger Aviary, literally hundreds of birds of various species chirping up a storm, we'd sit on a park bench to have a sandwich and maybe share a bottle of "Tizer" (our favourite if you remember) and finally, armed with fishing nets, went fishing by the side of the lake. I suppose we had a half dozen "Sticklebacks" between us in a Jam Jar of water before heading for the Tramcar and home. After a while, the Babysitter would leave us to our own devices until Mam got home. It was on one such occasion Bobby declared himself to be "very hungry" and promptly made some toast, which was a good idea, except some Sticklebacks also disappeared out of the jar. My Mam was a great believer in Castor Oil and so Bobby felt much better the following day.

There were times when Mam would leave me in the care of my Grandma who lived in Bond Street. I've learned that when she was a young girl she was a singer/ dancer in stage shows at the Stoll theatre on Westgate Road, (this theatre premiered "The Jazz Singer" starring Al Jolson the worlds first sound Movie). At one point she fell for and married a certain Tom White the owner of the show that she was in. The show was, "The Tom White Scandals", a little boy was born to them and they christened him "Samuel" (my Uncle Sam). Grandma's husband died after a while and some time later she remarried. Her new husband and she took the flat in Benwell.

Of course, by the time I was being looked after by my Grandma, she was in her seventies, and I myself would be around five years old. My mind retains certain images while I was with her. She was a great one for Tea of course, served with nice biscuits or perhaps a slice of chocolate Swiss Roll. I enjoyed this immensely, and I can see her in my minds eye now a velvet shawl, lace trim and so on as she pottered around the house. It was an upstairs flat typical of the area, and whenever I was there, she always seemed to have a pan of Stew on at the open fireplace and the big old black kettle forever on standby as she pottered about the house. I was intrigued. At times; sitting on her knee looking at her, fine pale complexion and her silver hair. The question I would ask her throughout the day was, "when's Mam coming home?" Her answer was the same each time: "Directly". It always sufficed.

In January of 1939, my new sister was born and she enjoyed the full attention of her two brothers and her sister. During that long hot summer, we took turns taking little Margaret in her new pram for walks in the street. Little did we know that our lives were to be changed forever in that same year by the savage that we all know as "Adolph Hitler". Soon war clouds were gathering and we were told that in all likelihood, the Germans would use poison gas against us, and so we were issued with Gas Masks. We learned how to put them on properly, then they were stowed in a cardboard box, with a piece of string attached to go over the shoulder and were instructed to carry them with us wherever we went. We began to practice and drill in the schoolyard in preparation for evacuation to Cumberland. Then families were notified of the date that we would actually leave and what we should expect. On the night before our departure, as Mam was going to be busy Bobby and I were sent off to the "Grand Cinema Palace" to see a brand new Movie called "The Wizard Of Oz".

Meanwhile, Mam packed our few pathetic belongings in pillow cases along with sandwiches and a bar of chocolate to see us through the journey, then the following morning off we went. I remember thinking at the time it seemed rather a silly idea, as I was certain I'd been "evacuated" in my left arm already by the doctor the previous year. Marching in two's we went down Canning Street, then past the Communal Wash House in Bond street used by folks to do the Family Wash (Bobby, as I recall had his arm in a plaster cast as he'd just broken his wrist a couple of days before,) Then on down Bond Street. As we passed my Grandma's house, I looked up and there she was, at her window crying, we waved. That was the last time I saw her. She died shortly afterwards, the noise of the air raids was too much for her. On Elswick Road beside the Bond Memorial Church were numerous tram cars, I'd never seen so many in one place before. We boarded at once and the teachers distributed themselves among the various groups of children on board and we moved off. Taken as far as Park road we all disembarked and were marched about a mile down this road to the Goods station, I wondered why it was that some folks on the street were at open windows waving at us and cheering, I then realized that somehow they knew what we were about, and of course we responded, waving back.

At the station a huge steam engine stood there coupled to numerous carriages, and was impatiently huffing and puffing steam all along the platform as porters opened carriage doors for us. A few intending passengers stood in groups looking at us and I noticed some with tears in their eyes. At the time I thought it strange because we kids reckoned it all rather a "hoot", mind you it may have been that these crafty folk had found out that we carried chocolate, lemonade and sandwiches in our luggage not to mention a few dolls and teddy bears or, in my case a favourite catapult. After all one never can tell with regards to Grown Ups. We were all marched into the carriages and dispersed throughout the various compartments, where arguments promptly ensued about who should have a window seat. A train whistle sounded, and with a sudden clanking jerk our train slowly moved off and began its journey westward. We traveled all day it seemed, the monotony broken only by our teachers and some volunteers moving about the train tending to the various needs of the children. On our arrival at "Home Saint Cuthbert's," a small village outside Carlisle, we were taken to a school used as a staging point before transporting children by road to their destinations. My brother and sister and I were taken by car to stay on a small farm owned by a Mr. and Mrs. Storey in a little village called Mawbray. Mam arrived with the baby the following day, and they were placed with a family just down The Street.

We learned a lot from our stay, and being "townies" we explored our new environment with zest. Up at 5:30 each day we helped to feed the calves, milk the cows, feed the hens (all after a fashion I might add). We were even taken with other children one morning on a horse and cart to "help" get the harvest in. We wore clogs which was a novelty to us, and being as young as we were, and from the City, we must have been more of a hindrance, and generally got in everyone's way. I recall pestering Mr. Storey to let me have a ride on a horse until one day he just grabbed me, sat me on "Blossom" a big black mare. He slapped her rump, and she took off across the meadow, with me, terror stricken, clinging to her mane. When she stopped, I slid off her back and decided right there that perhaps I would not make the same request of Mr. Storey, at least for a while.

Mam went home after a week or two with baby Margaret and Sister Sheila, it seemed the bombing had eased up and Dad after all was living alone, so Bobby and I were left to our own devices. We had a great time together with other boys from Newcastle, we were well fed and everyone at Storey's Farm was very kind. Lord knows, they were patient. For me though, the best moment at Mawbray, besides all the good times we had, was the afternoon that Bobby and I were sitting with our backs to the window in the tiny front room having our tea. Suddenly we heard a tapping on the window I spun around and there was dear old Dad's face peering in smiling, and waving, He'd come to take us home. Much hugging and chattering took place as we welcomed dad, then leaving him down stairs to talk to Mister Story, Bobby and I raced off to the bedroom to pack our things. I use the term "pack" very loosely as it must have taken us all of three minutes to do it. I also left the bedroom door ajar so that I could hear the voices droning on in the front room and know that dad had not left without us. The single deck bus for the journey home was, to my mind brought back from retirement and wheezed and rattled her gears all the way home. It didn't help having a blackout either with the mesmerizing scene of white lines painted on the road and telegraph poles as they whizzed past the window, with subdued lights and painted windows plus I was the only person without a seat. After a few miles someone, seeing my plight gave me a suitcase to sit on and then as darkness fell a kind lady insisted I rest my head on her knee, and I was asleep almost at once.

On our return to Newcastle, I attended Pendower School, as did Sheila and Bobby. Our schoolwork went on in dispersed with regular Air Raid drills trooping out to the new air raid shelters built in the schoolyard, where we sat singing songs at the behest of the teacher, or reciting the dreaded multiplication tables that we all loved so well. (Ahem). We boys thought it all a bit of a giggle really, or perhaps we were just being cavalier about it all, you must remember, there were girls in our class and after all "one must keep up appearances."

At home, we had an "Anderson" air raid shelter in the back garden (A design used all over the country). Made up of galvanized steel, corrugated for strength and sunk into the ground about three feet, leaving four feet above ground forming an arch above our heads then the whole thing was covered with earth. I learned that it was good protection for all but a "direct hit". As the sirens wailed Dad would pick us up from the bed and one by one took us downstairs to the shelter. After a while, if an air raid began, and the Bombing wasn't too close, we'd wait in the house a while,

Searchlights criss-crossed the sky and we'd sometimes see a German plane caught in the Beams then attacked by one of our fighters. The bomb explosions and the ack-ack fire were intense at times shaking the house and the noise was appalling, I guess that Parents all over put on a "good face" for the benefit of us kids. When daylight came, the boys of the neighborhood would race out to look for shrapnel, and when found, it was quite often still hot, we thought it great fun, but the local air raid warden was not at all amused. One particular day, whilst playing the game of Cowboys at the end of our street with a friend, we heard gunfire above us. His mother came running out, scooped him up under her arm, and as she ran she yelled that I should run home as the German plane in the sky was spraying bullets in our direction. I could never be described as fleet of foot, but that day, as I recall, I was quite exceptional.

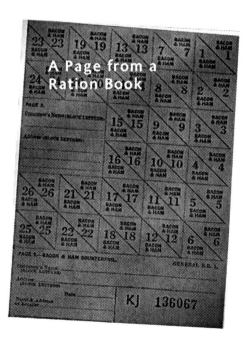

A Page from a Ration Book

Proper nutrition for children was of concern to the British Government at this time. What with the rationing of food, and fresh fruit being almost non existent, local authorities made available to each family a weekly jar of a nutritious mixture in the form of a sort of molten toffee, we kids loved it and would line up each evening to have a spoonful. Family ration books allowed a few ounces of cheese bacon and preserves per person among other things. Each family member was allowed one egg per week as part of his or her ration allotment and it was usually kept for Sunday morning Breakfast. However when Dad was asked if he'd like an egg he invariably answered "just give it to the Bairns" (children). Anyway Dad preferred his old favourite, toast, done at the coal fire and only toasted on one side. This last part was his idea from when we were small, he would do toast with a fork, on one side only, I guess with three children it was quicker that way, Oh! He was Irish all right. I grew up believing that this was the usual way that toast was made. If questioned on such behavior his retort would likely be, "Ah! But Jim, an Irishman is always allowed a second chance". At times, if he were miffed by a person's interference on the way he did things, without a pause he would respond, "An Irishman's always allowed to put the cart before the horse". I recall that more than once he admonished me, saying "why not take a civil walk around yourself then wake up and find yourself asleep" My father has always lived in my thoughts this way.

Because of the danger from bombing, all cities were "blacked out" and Newcastle was no exception. All windows were fitted with a black out blind of some kind; very few vehicles were on the road, because of the lack of petrol. Those that were, had only a one inch diameter circle of light coming from their head lamps, the rest was painted out, later, custom made hoods were fitted to headlights leaving only slits of light showing. Streetlights were not allowed of course, and bus and tram windows were painted, (as I said before) with a heavy blue paint.

There must be many stories of things that happened in the Blackout, (some of which we can't print here). Mam came home one night and told us that she came out of a store into the pitch-dark street and promptly collided with a lamp post. "Oh!" she said, "I do beg your pardon" then, embarrassed, hurried away into the seclusion of the Blackout. It truly felt that the world was about to sink into a pit of dark despair. The shining beacon that everyone clung to was the voice our Prime Minister, mister (now "Sir" Winston Churchill). One thing comes to mind about this turn of events; was that there were jobs galore for everyone. That is, everyone except lamplighters. Ironic, wouldn't you say?

It was about this time that the British Army was evacuated from Dunkirk, France. It was a disaster in many ways of course, one being that they had to leave behind all of their equipment. I was reminded of this early one Sunday morning as I waited at the Tram stop at the bottom of Pendower Way. Not a soul in sight, when to my amazement I saw across the street some men climbing furtively over the wall from the Benwell House Hotel grounds each one wearing a red arm band and carrying what I perceived to be a broom shank. As I stood there trying to decide whether to run or stay, I saw a man similarly equipped creeping from the bushes behind me wearing a blue arm band, he proceeded to point the broom shank across the street as

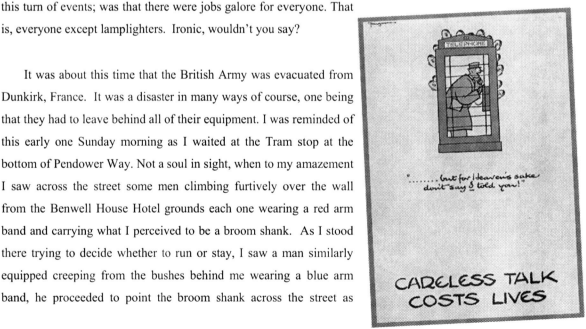

".........but for Heaven's sake don't say I told you!"

CARELESS TALK COSTS LIVES

though it were a Rifle, then he cried out "BANG". The result being that the Officer in charge across the street shouted to one of his men "OK Johnson you're dead, so stand over here"! It was of course the Local "Defense Volunteers" or the LDV (soon to become the "Home Guard"). They were in training to defend Britain, ("Should the invader come"), sans equipment.

Part of the national air defense in Britain was the use of barrage balloons; these were placed at strategic positions, and manned mainly by members of the Women's air force (WAAF). The nearest one to Pendower was stationed on some spare ground on Atkinson road in front of the library and could be seen at times tied down on this site for servicing. Its usual "stand by" position was about three hundred feet in the air, but when enemy planes were heading our way, it would ascend to a much greater height to ensnare them on their approach.

On a particular Sunday in 1943, a bad storm blew in from the coast just as the balloon barrage was on stand by. We kids watched from an upstairs window as our "local" balloon was thrown around in the sky, gas escaping all the while. It looked for all the world like a demented whale. Then it finally wrapped its steel cable around the steeple of our parish church tearing most of it off.

The bombing of Canny Newcastle became intense once again, so we were evacuated once more, just brother Bobby and I this time, to Wigton, a little Market town south of Carlisle. We stayed with a Mrs. Cox in William Street along with another Newcastle boy. In the beginning, we reported to a nice new school at the edge of town. Once in the schoolyard the Newcastle boys tended to congregate in one spot, studying "the lay of the land" I suppose. Brother Bobby was wearing a little tin badge on his lapel which read "Gang Buster" he'd got it from a packet of corn flakes back home) Just then a deputation of some local lads walked up and on seeing Bobby's badge the leader, asked "are you really a Gang Buster?" Bobby's nonchalant reply was "of course"; this prompted an immediate invitation to "join" the local gang, which we accepted. It pays to advertise I guess.

Soon we had to leave this school to avoid overcrowding, and were moved to a very old school in the high Street, loose floorboards all over the place and drafty as a barn. It was, I felt, actually due for demolition but what with the war, it was all there was available for us. Our teacher was a young red headed lady from our own school back home, a nice girl, she must have found out at an early stage that she could use a cane to punish her children in Cumberland and wasted no time in demonstrating her prowess with it. Oh! How her eyes would light up at the sound of the swish leaving livid red weal's on a little boy's hand, "Barbaric", I know because she gave me "two of the best" on each hand one day for the unspeakable crime of whispering in class. I remember trudging out into the play yard trying very hard to hold back the tears and failing miserably, I was angry with myself, for after all I was almost nine. However, that was many years ago, as for you dear lady, wherever you are, God Bless!

In the summer holidays Bobby and I were outdoors a lot with friends, there were fields and rivers aplenty. I learned to swim at a local indoor swimming baths, visited the stockyards at times to watch a pig being slaughtered and we were chased for our trouble by the Butcher, or, conversely, chased by an angry Sow around the Sty. The local High School was opened for our use to keep us out of trouble that included a fully equipped Gymnasium and a huge playing field.

It was on this field during a Cricket match that a friend of mine was injured when catching a ball, it hit him in the mouth knocking out his front teeth and he was taken to the local Hospital. Bobby, not to be outdone, decided that he would use the children's Slide in the local park whilst the park was closed, not only that, but he would go down backwards, unfortunately the park attendant in his "wisdom" had tied a chain across the bottom and Bobby just avoided breaking his neck. As it was, the chain caught him in the back, and it still gives him some jip to this day. In an attempt to occupy the time for the many extra children living in the area, the local Salvation Army opened their doors. Lots of the Newcastle boys and girls attended once a week in the evening, where we watched some movies sang songs and listened to some words from the Bible, very acceptable. A few miles away there was an Airport.

I was told that the runways were being extended, and to that end, a neighbour in our street who owned a truck was engaged to haul rocks and stones. In addition, to my joy I was asked if I would like to come along on a trip. We went first to a local rock quarry to load up with ballast thence to Kirkbride airport. I believe that I  talked for most of the trip, and my jaw must have dropped when we parked at the security gate mere feet away from a Wellington Bomber before dumping our load. The driver had to fill out forms while the security guard peered at me through the truck window, wondering if I was a German spy I suppose. After a while, we headed for home. It was my only trip. I assume the guy was glad to be rid of me and my constant questions.

When in town I would stand for what seemed hours at the entrance to a cavernous bus repair shed in town watching the huge red buses moving around, the sound of their Diesel engines filling the air drowning out all else around and Oh! The acrid smell of the exhaust, as some lucky chap reversed a huge snarling "Beast" over a pit in the floor and then commenced to climb down into it, clutching a tool box filled with "secret things". All this and I'm told they were paid for doing it. Filled with resolve I would wander back to William Street and did not even care if I was too late for tea!, A new Bus Driver in the making perhaps?

At one point Mam came to visit us at Mrs. Cox's house, it was a surprise to us and we spent the day walking and talking together then having lunch at William Street. As evening approached, Mam prepared to leave, but as Bobby was homesick Mam decided to take him with her, I felt very grown up as I took them to the bus stop to see them off. The Bus came and I bravely kissed Mam goodbye then watched as the Bus disappeared at the end of the road. It was with a feeling of sadness that I trudged back to the digs, the first time that I'd been left on my own so far from home.

Sometime later on my return to Newcastle I was greeted with the news that my favourite girl Dorothy had died, I was devastated and was numb for a long time afterwards. It was the first time in my young life that I'd been so close to a death, and for weeks afterwards I'd follow my Mother around the house as she was cleaning and dusting, asking "does this mean she's not coming back at all? Not ever?" For a very long time I harboured the hope that it was really a ghastly mistake and that one day when I went out to play I would see her once again. I was tormented by the fact that the previous summer, Dorothy and I had gone for a Sunday bus ride then a long walk right to Denton Dene to show her where I had once caught some frogs. The skies darkened and there was a frightful thunderstorm so we hurried home at once, we were of course soaked to the skin, she wore only a light summer dress and even though I had her wear my jacket around her shoulders it was to no avail. I always suspected that I had contributed to her demise.

During the war, Newcastle, being blacked out, as I mentioned earlier, no street lighting at all and of course rationing in effect, that, plus the bombing made for a pretty miserable life, but everyone although deprived were very cheerful. It brought out one of the most wonderful qualities of the British people: adjusting to new situations in times of adversity, and, to coin a phrase: "just Damn well getting on with it (excuse my French). People were to be seen every day in a line up outside various stores hoping to be able to buy most anything from bread to shoes, bananas to knitting needles.

Having the luxury of hindsight I can see now that there was humour to be found, like the time we got word that a certain shoe store actually *had* shoes for sale. I stood with Mam in the queue and waited, we reached the front and announced my dad's size, and colour in shoes that were required only to be told by the dour storeowner that he only had a larger size and in a different colour, adding that stuffing a little newspaper inside the toes would do the trick. Mam purchased them of course.

One evening Bobby and I set out to go to see a cowboy movie: "Western Union" at the "Rex" Cinema on Ferguson's Lane in old Benwell village, we were unable to get a seat for the "first Showing" of the evening, so we simply bought tickets for the second one. This meant we would not be home when we were expected, imagine our surprise when just as the main feature began, Dad himself walked in and sat down in the seat next to us, he'd come looking for his boys. Not wishing to spoil our evenings entertainment, he explained that he was "willing to wait" with us while we saw the movie. The upshot being that Dad got a free seat and thoroughly enjoyed the show as well.

The local Blind school was converted to a barracks for British troops and we kids went down there quite often and watched them drilling on the parade ground. The soldiers themselves were always cheerful and friendly I think they saw in us something of their own children at home. We were even allowed in the mess hall where the troops were eating, and were there when an officer came around shouting "any complaints? Usually this was followed by a voice at the back saying such things, as "you must be joking". We kids of course had what could be called an "Ulterior" motive as we hung around after the meal knowing that if we waited a while we would be offered a slab of fruitcake each.

Dad worked ten-hour days at Vickers Armstrong's factory on Scotswood Road and because of wartime conditions was not allowed to move to another job. Winter time was the worst as thinly clad he trudged to work through ice and snow, sometimes walking the whole distance as the buses were not running owing to the weather. Heaven only knows how he managed to negotiate the treacherous slopes of Gluehouse Lane leading down to his place of work. For all of this, which he did for his family, I salute him.

Christmas was always good;. Mam did wonders considering the state of affairs at the time. Around December time she would get a Credit coupon from Cooks of Saville Row in the City, it was a store that would extend credit to folks such as us whose income was nothing to write home about. The tallyman would call every Saturday morning for a small amount to repay the loan, yes and there were some Saturdays when Mam barely had enough to cover it. How humiliating for her, though it was common enough with folks at that time where we lived, but I digress. Mam would take us in the tram to "Cookes" Department Store, it was quite an adventure, and she'd select clothes for us all then we'd visit Santa Claus in the toy department, we'd ogle the toys of course but we were always told not to touch. I guess that while we were occupied, Mam's orders for Christmas goodies were whispered over the counter. Traditionally, the larger stores in town would open a "Santa's grotto" for children. We would troop in on command, visit Santa, and receive a small gift. Mam paid for it of course. One year at age seven, I was mistakenly given a gift meant for a much older child. I opened it on the bus and was filled with remorse. At home my dad uttered some choice words about their stupidity, grabbed his coat and hurried out into the night. He was back in a short while clutching a toy wind up motor bike and sidecar for me. The rest of the evening was spent chasing this article around the floor, much shrieking and giggling from us all. Dad had once again saved the day.

The days leading up to Xmas were, as always, ones of great anticipation, planning, and hiding away of mysterious packages, Mam spent time baking bread, scones and suchlike, preparing things like Xmas puddings, hanging decorations and so forth, Myself, I wished I could just go to bed, and wake up on Xmas morning, the pain was so great. I do remember with great fondness a scene one evening, of the room lit only by the candles on the tree, beside which, Mam, holding Baby Margaret, Softly sang "Silent Night".

Xmas Day was of course a day of magic, even now I can smell the delicious aromas emanating from the kitchen, a special effort was made by the Ministry of Food to get some Goodies from overseas into the shops prior to Xmas. (The tragedy is that it was only later in life that I realized that so many brave men died at sea bringing the British people the means to have a nice Christmas). Early morning our Christmas stockings would reveal an orange and an apple each, also nuts and some chocolate (Cadburys of course). We even had an imitation tree about three foot tall standing on the sideboard, the room gaily decorated with streamers of various shapes and sizes, the fire burning brightly and we kids playing with our toys on the floor. At times, we would have a nice surprise as our cousins from South Shields: Jesse and Iris (teenagers by then) would pay us a Christmas visit. Dad thought the world of the girls and would stop whatever he was doing to talk to them. Dad usually did the job of cooking the Midday meal on weekends, and Christmas day was no exception. At the risk of repeating myself, I'll tell you that, as I write, I can see in my minds eye, my Dad, with a dish towel over his shoulder, checking the Roast in the oven, or as we all sat at the table he'd carry in five plates of food balanced on one arm. Showing his prowess as a waiter I guess. Well Done Dad! Strange thing is, Dad preferred to have very little food at midday, but really enjoyed the roast "cold" in the evening with a drop of Hot Mustard.

Before long the bombing started again and Bobby and I were evacuated once more, this time to Hexham, it was a place named "Dukes House Boys Camp". Bobby tells of the time that Dad came to visit him, it was Christmas I believe; he was carrying a book on Bobby's favourite film "Pinocchio", a new Disney production. Arriving by bus in Hexham he had to walk two miles uphill to the camp, it was raining heavily and Dad did not have a raincoat but undaunted he pressed on, after a while a car pulled up and the driver offered dad a lift, he accepted thankfully only to find that the camp gates were all of 100 yards away. This not withstanding Bobby really enjoyed having the book. Many thanks Dad!

On my arrival at the camp, I was put in the same dormitory with Bobby and was given the bunk above his. The ten dormitories were named after trees, ours was called the "Poplars", there was even a little six-bed Hospital called the "Sycamore" (get it?) Oh! Very droll.   We had many good times together there, although it was run rather on Army lines, up at six each morning and into the wash house for a cold wash then back to tidy up the bunks. Each one had to be made up exactly right, blankets folded in a particular manner and the locker spick and span with each boy standing at attention at his bed space by the time the whistle blew. On my first morning I was standing there when our house master (late of Canning St School) came on his inspection tour swinging his three tailed leather belt, beady eye flicking from bunk to bunk.   Then, Oh! Heaven forbid! One of my blankets on the top bunk was somewhat awry. For this flagrant violation, I was given the belt on my hand. It caused me much pain of course but what I could not understand was why a new boy like me could be found guilty of such a thing on the spot when no one had told me of these stringent rules. I look back and realize we were all playing soldiers. The teachers were the officers of course.

There was a school at the camp, but first we were marched down to the dining hall for breakfast, the food was good and it seemed to me that there was plenty of it. Next to the Dining Hall was a small "Tuck Shop" which was open for an hour or so each day, pies, cakes and a small assortment of sweets, very popular with the boys, that is, when we had any money. Mam generally sent us a Shilling or two when she could, but, for the life of me, looking back, I do not know how she managed to do it.

At Suppertime one of the teachers, a Mr. Mathews would at times be on duty in the dining hall where he would stand on a small stool to supervise.   We liked him because he would tell us stories; about a character that was forever in a scrape of one sort or another, his name, "Geordie" and it was always a Story that made us laugh. From time to time after climbing into bed, one of the older boys would sit by the pot-bellied stove and read a Story aloud to us all, although to be honest I do not remember hearing the end of most of them. My Parents, as I think I've said before would often be heard to say, "Young Jimmy could sleep on a clothes line" .On fine days groups of boys would be marched off into the surrounding country-side for a bracing hike singing songs as we went and although we were tired when we returned we all agreed that it was preferable to sitting in a stuffy classroom. On Saturday afternoons we were allowed to go into town, often to the pictures or to buy pens and pencils, writing paper, soap, comics (if funds would allow).   We were also told of the places that were "off Limits". It was, overall a great experience for me and I believe my stay at the camp has stood me in good stead.

Of course, it was not all a bed of roses; something came along to take me out of the picture. Cases of Diphtheria were found in the camp and the whole place was put into quarantine. Along with some other boys, I was identified as being a "Carrier" of diphtheria, which means that we were not ill with it, we just "carried" it around in our puny little bodies. In any event, we were promptly whisked off to the camp hospital and there we waited for an ambulance.   We were taken to an Isolation hospital in Newburn for a few weeks, a very cold, and a very boring stay I might add. Mam came to see me at one point in the middle of a snow storm I remember looking out of the window and there she was, snow piled on top of her hat walking in the blinding snow.

The shame was that we were not allowed to actually meet, but to look at each other through a window inside the ward Mam in the office and me sitting on the edge of a bed in the ward. I might say that I could have used a hug that day. It was quite a severe winter, never the less each day after lunch we boys were sent outside to walk in the hospital grounds. Part of our treatment I suppose and one of the reasons I christened it an "*Ice*"-olation hospital. After a while we boys, one by one were declared fit and sent home, and I believe I detected a look of relief on the face of more than one nurse A most patient and dedicated staff as ever one could wish for.

Dad had to work some ungodly hours during the war, it being a Munitions factory, and he would arrive home dead tired at about seven o'clock only to find it was his turn for "fire Watch" on our block for a couple of hours. Shortly after going to bed he would have to get up if there was an air raid, of course he was not alone in this, and all men living at home were pressed into service to watch for possible falling incendiary bombs.   One particular evening about nine thirty or so I was sitting by the fire with Dad, he was reading the paper, when quite suddenly he leapt to his feet with a cry, I asked him what on earth was the trouble, and was told there was something he'd left undone at work, grabbing his coat he headed for the door. I went with him and as we hurried to the Bus stop at the top of Hodgkin Park Road he explained that as he left his work, his job was to switch off the furnace and on that night he had forgotten to do it, bear in mind that it was long before the sophisticated Electrical controls we have today.

On leaving the bus, we hurried down Glue house Lane and whilst I waited at number twenty-eight Security gate, Dad went inside with a cheerful "Good Evening Tom" to the Guard. I remember this incident mainly because it was one of the few times that I was with Dad and had him all to myself. When dad returned to where I waited we found that the bus service was finished for the evening so we rode in the Tram Car along Scotswood road and into the Town centre. Then we walked up Westgate Road to the "Big Lamp", turning left along Elswick Road to Pendower, quite a walk, considering that My Dad always walked at a fast pace and I had to keep up with him. I would complain at times like these that my legs ached. Dad would say "growing pains Jimmy, just growing pains" As I think I've said before, Dad was first and foremost , an Irishman.

Not too long after this, a friend and I were going to the "Pictures" in Benwell but we found on our arrival that it was sold out. This presented a problem, no matter, we simply jumped onto a tram and rode into the city, and went to the Stoll movie house to see "The adventures of Tartu" starring Robert Donat It was a good show but I was unaware of the worry I caused my parents. It was after ten o'clock when I stepped off the tram where my father was standing waiting with the local Constable, I was taken across the road and into the Police box where I was given a severe talking to on the folly of my ways. I did not repeat any thing like that again

As a boy, I was often envious of other kids when I saw them riding their bicycles around and thought how convenient it must be to own one. Imagine my delight when one day when I was about eleven years old, Peter, my friend from along the street, let me borrow his older brothers Raleigh roadster Bicycle to ride around in the street, this was a great Idea except that his brother was a grown man. Undaunted, I only knew I had the use of a bike, so I rode around our street with my right leg protruding through the frame to the right pedal, bobbing up and down as I went. It must have looked grotesque to say the least and not a little dangerous, "But Man! I was cycling".

In Pendower by this time, even I could see that the War had taken its toll. People were fed up, but we kids just got on with it as we did not feel the strain of rationing and shortages or even the threadbare clothes we wore. About this time, my best friends were Cecil, Richard and Edwin, boys who also went to Pendower school, we were at the "adventure" stage in our lives we talked and dreamed of "Daring Do" on the High Seas hidden treasures etc. (for Richard and Edwin, at least some of their dreams came true, as Richard later joined the Merchant Navy and Edwin, the last I heard was in the Canadian Navy). Cecil unfortunately was a lad with a heart condition from birth and was obliged to play the quieter games, but later became active in the Salvation Army, Well done lads! We had such a good time together. I recall quite vividly the time we decided that we should conquer the world (as no one had done it recently!)

Before the war November the Fifth being Guy Fawkes Day was a busy one for us children, the main task was to build a "Bon Fire". Lots of fuel would be needed hence children could be seen dragging old tree stumps, carrying anything from bits of old furniture, to dry leaves looking very much like ants at work. There was Piracy of course, as some boys and girls would purloin things from one prepared fire to feed their own, I have even seen battles ensue. When darkness came the fireworks began, Catherine Wheels, Jumping Jacks, Roman Candles and of course Rockets. Bobby was apparently curious about the "thrust" of a given Rocket and decided to find out first hand, (no pun intended) he held one by the shaft and lit the blue touch paper. Consequently, the Royal Victoria Infirmary had an extra patient to care for that night. During the war, of course, there were "no fireworks" as such and bon fires were out of the question.

Winters in the North East could be wicked but all of us young' uns saw it simply as a change of style and we eagerly adapted to suit. When the snow came we would create long icy slides in the street or in the school yard, but best of all was the sledge run we had on SunnyBank Avenue, This was a street which ran down from Bertram Crescent to Benwell Lane, scores of kids came to use it bringing their Sledges including Bobby and I. One small detail comes to my mind; Benwell Lane was a Main Bus route. The sledges would just swing 90 degrees at the bottom of the street and hopefully come to a stop. Occasionally a concerned resident living down there would sneak out at the dead of night, spread ashes, and salt at the end of the run, Lord! Only knows how many lives he saved. But to us, when we discovered the heinous crime we certainly thought of reporting it to the Police. Bobby's sledging fun was interrupted one afternoon when a car came out of a side street, and turned down the street where Bobby was sledging someone shouted a warning, Bobby looked behind as he raced downhill in time to see the car's front bumper, then everything went black; Mam called the Doctor in.

Our School Teachers, for the most part had been brought out of retirement because younger men and women teachers were now serving in the forces. Our Head Master, Mr. Lee, introduced a middle aged lady teacher to our class one day and explained that we'd have to speak up as she was " hearing impaired", on his departure a chuckle went around the class as we realized what a good time we'd have now. Without speaking she walked to the blackboard and wrote the number 40 in the corner "That's how many years I've been teaching children like you" she said in a very loud voice. Followed by "and I know tricks you haven't even thought of yet" then added, "I may be deaf but I'm not daft" She then turned and said "now, let us begin" from that moment we revered her and were her slaves forever.

Miss Harrison was a "card" she was our Art and Drama teacher and one of my certain favourites, she quite often picked me out for a role in one of her productions. I was always flattered of course, that is until she chose me one day to demonstrate my acting abilities. I was to walk clear across the room to propose Marriage to a perfectly innocent girl sitting there. I walked over to where she sat, feeling about the size of a mouse. As I stood there, literally squirming. The rest of the class promptly collapsed in Hysteria, the girls face turned bright red as I shuffled my feet, and stared at the floor, all this and not a word spoken. Finally, just as I wished that I could pass out or anything at all, to free me of this torment, Miss Harrison spoke: "Well Done, James! Very believable, you may go back to your desk".

35

School concerts were very popular, usually put on at the end of term, and I must say that Miss Harrison's class had some very fair talent to offer. One of our boys, Les, was a great pianist; he'd play everything from Jazz to the Classics, Actors galore and of course quite a few Dancers. My favourite act was a pretty girl named Sheila; she would dress up as "Carmen Miranda" a famous Hollywood star at that time and sing songs with a Latin touch. At such events the headmaster "Mr. Lee" would sit in the front row looking very stern, a paragon of propriety, but on one occasion this was to be strained to its limits. Miss Harrison arranged that during one of her songs Sheila was to sing directly to Mr. Lee; the song, "I Like You Very Much", it was delivered with great feeling, I've never seen a man squirm so much, still, he was a good sport about it and led the applause.

Speaking of squirming, one middle-aged woman teacher gave the class an assignment to do an essay. The title she decided would be "The Alarm Clock" and that we could do it from any point of view. I thought that my creativity came to the fore that day and when I was finished I was quite proud of my work. Two days later, I was called to her desk where she proceeded to bully me in front of the class. She said she had read the story I had submitted and told me that it was obvious that it was not my work. Further, she said that "I must admit at once that I'd gotten it from a Text Book!". Well folks, as I saw her bloodshot eyes glaring at me, I was certain that she was going to actually strike me. My courage to protest failed me, so I meekly admitted my guilt in this Dastardly Deed. The essay was however, my own creation! (The lads got talent!). "Where ever you are Miss, I forgive you".

Ambiguities notwithstanding, I regained my self-esteem a short while later whilst in the schoolyard. A class monitor ran up to tell me I was to report to my home teacher (Miss Harrison) right away. Trying to remember any misdemeanors I had hanging over me I duly complied. She was in the classroom in a high state of excitement about an essay, which I had done the previous week. All the students in class had been told to do a few pages on National Savings and its importance in the scheme of things at that time of War. My humble effort, (according to her) was quite Churchillian. So much so that I was requested to read it out to the entire school Assembly two days hence. I acquiesced of course.

At twelve years old I fell in love whilst in this class with a girl by the name of Norma, it was unrequited of course. Heck, she didn't know that I existed. I found out that at least three other boys were of the same mind. Maybe that was the reason I turned to comedy. One routine was the use of black paper placed across my front teeth to give the impression of a gap. First I displayed this to the boy on my left, who giggled aloud followed by the whole class; the hysterics of the class was cut short by Miss Harrison's voice telling me "A good Comedian does *not* prolong a good joke young man!" I knew then that I'd have trouble getting a booking on the Halls.

I was sitting at the back of the class one day, the teacher had gone to see the headmaster about something, and we had been left to read. I noticed half a dozen girls in a huddle at the front of the class. Quite suddenly, one of them jumped up and cried out "if you must Know, John Smith and I *had it* last night." The class became deathly quiet and I wondered what it was that they had. Of course, it being wartime everything was in short supply. I thought maybe they had bought something on the black market. Someone asked for details but she would not say. One boy in the class asked this John Smith for information in the schoolyard, and got a fat lip for his trouble, it was all very mysterious I thought.

Because of food shortages, the Ministry Of Food encouraged us to create a vegetable garden. Dad dug over the front lawn and part of the back, planted potato and lettuce while I was given a few feet of ground to bring forth some peas and carrots, no one was more surprised than me when after a few weeks I sat in our kitchen shelling those peas, but the carrots? The less said the better. Dad got quite a lot of potatoes from his plot but some were washed away in a weekend storm, ah well! We tried.

On Sundays, Bobby and I would take turns going up to our Aunt Sarah's house in Canning Street Benwell to wash the linoleum floor as she was unable to do so herself. And Oh! The rewards, it was a different atmosphere, no brothers or sisters competing for attention, Uncle Jack and Aunt Sarah all to myself. After chores were done we'd have lunch, Roast Beef and Yorkshire pudding etc. but cooked just a little differently and a lovely dessert (or Sweet as we used to call it). All for "little old me" . . . then reading and talking by a nice fire, I even got to use the outside lav. down the stairs in the back yard. I would read by the fire in the afternoon and soon enough it was teatime, and what a spread! Sandwiches, cakes, trifle. Even mixed fruit and cream, however, again I digress, all too soon it was time to go, perhaps clutching a coin from Aunt Sarah, but not before listening to "Children's Hour" on the B.B.C. A fond memory indeed. I always think of those times whenever I come across the poem by James Whitcomb Riley called "Out to old Aunt Mary's".

I applied for, and got, a job as a "Paper Boy" at Cairn's newspaper shop on Bertram Crescent, which was only five minutes walk from our house. Brother Bobby was already a paper boy there; it paid Six shilling and sixpence a week (a Kings Ransom to me at that time). My route took me the entire length of Bertram Crescent, Wiedner road, Denhill Park and all points between. It meant up with the lark every day for my morning round, then evening deliveries after school and of course the Sunday papers.

Mornings were special to me, more so if it was Winter, all sound muffled by the snow, moonlight showing the furtive figure with the red nose, blowing on his fingers for warmth, slipping at times, but, recovering in time to put the Newspaper in the appointed letterbox. Most windows were in darkness, but those souls whose work awaited them were astir, and the window, sometimes showed a crack of light through the blackout curtains, this was a welcome sight to our morning traveler. A time or two a person would come to the door, eager to receive the paper and the benevolent early riser might offer me Tea, or perhaps even a bacon sandwich, which I would gladly accept then hurry on my way refreshed. At the end of the week, I would hand over my wages to Mam, and she would give me one shilling and sixpence back, I think she must have felt like "Christmas".

Within a few months Bobby and Sheila left school, Bobby took a job as office boy in Vickers Armstrong's Factory, and Sheila became a shop assistant in Fenwick's, a very smart Department store in Northumberland Street, Newcastle. After a year or so at my paper delivery job I took on a better paying one: twelve shillings a week for delivering green groceries on Friday evening and all day Saturday for a green grocer's shop which was situated at the top of Atkinson road. Firstly, the orders had to be made up for delivery and the bills made out, we even boiled our own beetroot in the cellar.

When all orders were in their respective wooden boxes, I'd load them onto a handbarrow and get on the road. It was a daunting route, as I think back of the steep hills involved: Bishops Road, Hodgkin Park Road, and Benwell Grange Road. In the snow too, I don't know how it was that I didn't lose a load not to mention how it was a lad my size could push the dratted thing back up those same hills, anyhow twelve Bob was not to be sniffed at.

Mam was so pleased that there was finally an increase in the income to the family, but it was to be short lived, you see the War was just winding down and after all who needs workers in a munitions factory in time of peace? Therefore, my Dad was among the hundreds layed off. It was during his layoff that I went with him when he went for a walk. He really liked walking, and as dad would say "it costs nothing." A time or two he would meet someone he knew and was often asked how he was doing. His reply was cavalier to say the least: "Oh! I'm a Gentleman Of Leisure *now*", he would reply. Somehow, at the time it gave me a lump in my throat.

At the War's end I felt rather strange as I realized that I would be able to go into a shop and buy sweets whenever I wanted, Mam would go on a shopping spree that would never end, I even wondered where I could borrow a wheelbarrow. Of course, I was well intentioned, but I was not to know that Britain was bankrupt after the turmoil of the war. Much time would pass before controls such as rationing would disappear. We would have some years of austerity yet. The British people would have to close ranks once again and bite the bullet. It could be confusing for a lad such as me. For when sweets were finally taken off the ration, I dashed into a shop, intending to clear at least one shelf of chocolate. I was clutching a hand full of useless sweet coupons. However, I did not have a penny to my name. (Exit left) At this time it was all too common to see a man going to his place of work very obviously wracked with pain from wounds he had received in the war,

Boarding a bus with difficulty and of course it was usually crowded but there was no shortage of passengers offering their seats to him. At this time food rationing became even more severe, and just to sweeten the pot, America cancelled the Lend Lease program for Britain. This coupled with bomb damage repair told us we had a long row to hoe.

It was not too long before Dad got a job in his old position as Waiter at the "Turks Head" Hotel in town. All of the family was pleased for him now that he was out of that miserable place known as Vickers Armstrong's factory. I remember him having a tough time scrubbing and manicuring his hands to get them in good condition for his new job. We could all tell he was excited about prospects, and I knew he had earned his chance, having "paid his dues" so to speak. He would often tell us after his day's work about some of the famous Actors, Comedians, and Singers that he had both served and spoken with that day, There is no doubt that Dad's folksy manner and natural Irish charm served him well. Stars who stayed at the Hotel (when they performed at the "Palace" or the "Empire Theatre") included George Formby, Max Wall, Nat Mills and Bobby, Cavan O'Connor, and the North's all time favourite Comedian; Frank Randal. Heaven only knows how many more.

Dad's favourites were the very successful Irish team "Arthur Lucan and Kitty McShane" (Old Mother Riley and her daughter Kitty from Dad's home town of Dublin) he was thrilled to bits when these performers told him that he must always be the one to tend their table. I myself saw these Artistes a number of times in the theatre and the Movies in our area and they became my favourites too.

Our tramway system in Newcastle was due to be scrapped in 1939 but was postponed because of the War, now the wreckers were moving in. The Trams were to be replaced by trolley Buses. It was, I must say, like losing a friendly and well loved member of the community and I for one, get a little Misty eyed when I look at pictures of them. I thank Heaven that places like the open air Museum at "Beamish" near Newcastle has renovated a number of them. They are there, for all to see and enjoy.

Festivities in the streets greeted the end of the war of course and by now I had been transferred to Whickham View Secondary School for my last year of formal education. I had at this time a collection of newspaper pictures of Generals on both sides, Aircraft, ships, etc. even of the infamous German prison camps. I had an album of film stars, many leggy ones too; I guess I was growing up. Our teacher was "quite a guy" he was short in stature but ruled his class with a rod of iron as it were. He would be looking over the work that some unfortunate soul had handed in when quite suddenly he would fling the book clear across the room yelling " Your work is " STINKING BAD SIR". For the next few minutes the whole class would be trying to suppress giggles without being caught, looking back I do believe he was just trying to entertain us.

It was at this place that I met a lad, Bill by name who lived in Denton Burn, not far from the school, so Glen and I would go down by bus to see him in the evening and in so doing met two very canny lasses, Doreen and Ruth, I was to know them only a short while before Doreen and family immigrated to Australia but although Ruth took up some very serious Ballroom dancing in the city, her and I would meet again and renew our acquaintance later. We all drifted apart, that is until Bill and I met again in North Wales a few years later.

Christmas 1945, time for me to leave regular school and make my own way in the World. A Xmas party was arranged to be held in the girls section of the school, boy's were paired off with a girl partner for the evening and instructed how we must sit her at the table, "dance" with her and attend to her every whim. Well we boys, to put it mildly would have rather got stuck into the grub, and let the girls dance by themselves, but we did our best, and the evening went quite well, considering that our teacher even treated us to a song. (Oh, My Gawd!)

As 1946 arrived, I began work as a pre. Apprentice Electrician at contractors named Sleigh and Woods situated in North Street in the city, my wage was to be one pound, one shilling and six pence, I was so proud and was walking on air as I handed Mam my pay packet at the end of that week. I'm not really sure why I decided to be an Electrician, it was the way in those days to follow in Fathers footsteps, but I just wanted some thing a little better for myself. To begin with, I was put in the store, which was a sort of loft upstairs above the office. I was given some busy work to do, but first I was to assist the electricians to get out the supplies they needed for the various projects they were involved with. Then came the great day when I was assigned to an electrician to go to Chester-Le Street to work on some renovation work at a club there. Firstly the man told me that I was to carry the tool box as we walked to the bus station. I used both hands to do what he asked but it felt as though it were nailed to the floor and I failed to budge it. Joe, recently out of the Army, just smiled and observed; as he hoisted it effortlessly onto his shoulder with one hand "You'll need to get a few pot pies inside you first Jim". It was interesting, of course and I was just the flunky, fetch and carry etc,

However, I found that I enjoyed going all over the city and beyond on various jobs from installation work, to repair jobs on ships berthed in the River Tyne. On one memorable day two of us apprentices were sent carrying a triple extension ladder for an electrician to the "Eldon Grill", an upscale bar in the town center to replace a faulty portion of the neon sign. Once the ladder was in place the electrician blithely told me to go inside the building whilst he climbed the ladder up to the third floor. I was to go upstairs, through the kitchen and simply step out of the window onto an 18-inch wide ledge to assist him in his work. His only words to me were "don't look down". Utterly brilliant . . Sending a fourteen year old novice on such a job. I sidled along that ledge hardly daring to breathe never mind look down. While shuffling back to the window, my foot caught on one of the many wires, lying at my feet I froze, and a bolt of sheer terror shot through me. I finally got back to the open window and literally fell into the room. It was right then and there that I made a solemn promise to myself that it was the last time that I would ever let myself be put in harms way, especially by what I would call, an absolute moron.

One day I was sent with an Electrician to fix a problem aboard a ship on her degaussing gear. This was the system installed on ships during the recent war to repel magnetic mines at sea. At that time, there were still thousands of them out there. I was able to roam all over the ship and whilst on the bridge I recall being sorely tempted to ring down for "full ahead both engines". For the most part the Electricians working for this contractor were recently out of the armed services and seemed a pretty easy going bunch, although I had the distinct impression that after wearing a uniform, being pushed around, and told what to do, anyone giving them a hard time would get a Black eye.   After a few months, I left and went to work for an Electrical Supplier in Handyside's Arcade in Percy Street.

My job was behind the counter serving various people from electrical contractors in the City, but my favourite task was Pick up and Delivery around Newcastle. I was given a big old Bicycle with a simply huge carrier basket on the front, (" the accent here is on "the old") there was no consideration given to load stability whilst riding it I'm afraid and I came a cropper a couple of times. There would be coils of wire rolling down the street, car horns honking, as I stumbled around to retrieve the merchandise and the melodious cries of car drivers as they gave forth with vituperative language. The brakes had unfortunately seen better days, and it brought me into trouble with the law at least once. I recall vividly the day that I turned from Pilgrim Street into Mosley St; it dips quite steeply to the intersection of Dean Street where in the middle of the Road stood a big beefy policeman on Point Duty. His outstretched arm told me to halt! However, my brakes said, "No can do". As I finally rolled to a halt, the Constable approached and inquired, "How long I'd been in the fire Brigade?" I explained that "the brakes were a problem" and he promptly wrote up a warning to the company. On my return to the shop, my name was "Mud" of course, after all "who the Hell does this lad think he is? ("Asking for brakes on the bike, indeed").

Most Newcastle folk are familiar with characters who sometime or other lived, in the area, such as "Tommy on the Bridge" who in the 1930's could be seen standing in all kinds of weather on the High level bridge across the river Tyne. Well, in wandering about Newcastle on that bike I became aware of a couple myself, one was a lady in the Grainger Market who cried out her wares outside a small cafe in order to attract customers. "Nice Rabbit dinners hinny, nine pence up or doon, sweet green oranges Pet, take ya pick. Penny a bunch the mint bonny lad", or "boiled egg and a biscuit there's seats gannin beggin". It seemed that her voice would reach you wherever you might be in the market.

Another lady stood all day in Grainger St. Always dressed in black and quite old as I remember, She'd stand huddled in wind and rain against a buttress in the wall of a bank without any sign of discomfort. She seemed to be clutching a package under a voluminous cloak. I never did find out what she was selling but every so often, a man would sidle up and money would change hands in exchange for merchandise. Business is business so they say.. I left the delivery job after a few months and resumed my apprenticeship again this time nearer home. It was at this time that I discovered that lots of girls were to be found at Dances. This led to my going to the local Parish Hall, Atkinson road on Saturday nights along with my friends Glen, Brian, Bill and Allen. Mind you! We did not *have a clue how to dance*, but we went anyway. The boys seemed to favour standing on one side of the room, the girls on the other. It was pathetic really, a boy would ask a girl to dance and sometimes, (Horror of Horrors) the girl would refuse. I've seen it happen and the boy would stand there, "destroyed". Ah the pains of growing up. Slowly as the night wore on, couples would get together and the dance floor would fill up.

The gentleman who was M.C. and I believe was also the organizer of the dance, we knew only as Pop, he would stand at times in front of the band and sing, mostly numbers like "When You're Smiling", and other songs of the day. A good Baritone, he stood erect with a small song book held in both hands in front of him, very proper! If some young man held his partner in any other than the correct way while dancing, you could bet that "Pop" would walk right up to them and say "ere, 'ere, none of that!" "If yer can't dance properly then kindly leave the floor!" I myself ventured on to the floor but only for a Bradford Barn dance, which allowed a person to dance some simple repeating steps with most everyone on the floor, always good for small talk and perhaps a giggle. It was then that I decided to take a few lessons and did so at our local youth club.

I met my first serious girl friend at a Saturday night Hop in the same Parish Hall; her name was Joan, a pretty girl, very friendly and easy to talk to. One night I got up courage to ask her for a date, and so it was that we went to see "Red River", a Western starring John Wayne (who else?) at the "Plaza" on the West road. Not altogether a happy time though, as when I got home I realized that I must have dropped my last ten shilling note on the floor in the Theatre.

After a near sleepless night I hurried up there and arrived as the cleaning ladies were sweeping up in the various rows of seats in the auditorium, I explained my problem to them and going to the area where I'd sat, I saw the note on the floor smiling up at me. I was much relieved I can tell you and with the applause of the cleaning staff ringing in my ears and the note safely in my pocket I headed back home. Joan and I went steady for a couple of years, and we had some good times together, her family always made me welcome and we got on very well, then we just seemed to drift apart.

My job this time was in Benwell, A guy by the name of Andy had opened a small Electrical Contracting outfit just opposite the Adelaide Picture house on Elswick Road he had only one electrician, Dave, and he needed an apprentice (this was his lucky day, was it not?) Dave was a real nice guy although I thought him very old, good Heavens, he was twenty-eight! He and I got on O.K. he had a great sense of humour and I learned a lot from him.

I dread to think what he thought of me at times, being a typical teenager, but he persevered and I guess he saw me grow. I worked with Dave doing Electrical installations of varying types and sizes all over the North East (I believe we installed hundreds of fluorescent lights in Newcastle area alone) and various jobs from Whitley Bay to Wylam, from Burradon Colliery to West Hartlepool Pool. I was required to work for a couple of weeks on night shift in town at Fenwicks department store the reason 'for night shift "was so that we could climb about using tools and ladders etc without disturbing anyone. I recall feeling very grown up getting nightshift pay. As time went on some other Electricians and Apprentices joined the Fray and the business grew.

One Electrician I liked working with was Jackie. He was special, he told me about his life growing up and some of his achievements, and I admired him a great deal, as he was accomplished in many fields. Jack was quite the philosopher, one Saturday morning as I cleared up our tools at a job we were involved with Jack spoke: "Jim" he said, "I know you tell me about how you are having a great time, traveling all over the place, meeting girls etc. well "watch out" before you know it you'll be much older. You will wonder where the time went". "You were right on the mark Jack". Mind you ,I learned a lot as I went along.

I found that I *enjoyed* moving around on various jobs in Newcastle, and yes, we met many canny folks and each job presented its own Problems and Delights. One regular customer for us Was Backly's Bakery situated in the high street in Wallsend. I well remember the day that Dave the electrician told me to go and make a can of tea for break time. I knew the routine by heart as I did this chore every day, and so grabbing the tea can I made my way through the labyrinth of departments to get water at the sink in the store room, thence to the gas ring situated inside an adjacent Bathroom. I pushed open the bathroom door and there before me, was the manager of the retail store of the Bakery. To my surprise, she was engaged in activity that people *usually were engaged in* at such times. She gave a squeal, and I got such a fright that I dropped the can of water on the floor, and to put it succinctly, I scarpered. I explained to Dave's surprise that I wasn't in the mood for tea that day and would rather "have a smoke" outside. Later in the day I finally got up enough courage to speak to the lady in question. I found her in her office and after a timid knock on the door was told to enter. Red faced I offered my profound apologies, at which point she assured me that the blame rested with herself for failing to close and lock the door, and I was to think no more about it. She then poured tea for us both, and assured me that we were still friends. All grist for the mill I suppose!

I was sent as an apprentice with an electrician called to do an installation job in Pilgrim Street in town. Jimmy was also his name, _ he liked his beer and each day, as soon as the pubs were open he would lay out some work for me and off he'd go. The Boss would visit the site after hours to check on progress and the following day when I called at the shop to pick up supplies for the job he would read the riot act to me for not pushing things ahead enough. Jimmy was incensed when he heard of this and promptly called at the shop the following morning himself where he proceeded to tear a large strip off the Boss saying that he should be man enough to go to the source if he had something to say about the job. He added that "young Jim was the best apprentice in the shop if he did but realize it". I walked out of the shop three feet off the ground that day. I did not know it then but I was to meet Jimmy again a few years later on a construction site at Consett Steel works.

A boy I went to school with by the name of Alan and myself decided that we should cycle to Jedburgh in Scotland, on a week end, some sixty miles and I was riding a single speed bike, hilly terrain and a strong wind did not help either. Ah! Foolhardy Youth! It was quite pleasant as we set out, but as we progressed over the "Cheviot Hills", a steady rain came down. It came to me; at least it became apparent to my legs that a single speed bike was; perhaps, only good for carrying sacks of coal. Alan did have the advantage on his bike of numerous gears, and I suggested we swap after a while, just to give me a break, but he did not agree, I think maybe I created a record of some sort, I could just imagine the Headlines) in the local newspaper. "Local boy makes good on "stormy trip to Jedburgh" Scotland on single speed bicycle". (Although he's expected to live). A long climb faced us to finally reach the border, and "Carter Bar" awaited us at the top. As we began our ascent, the rains came, along with a steady wind, which moaned through the trees, and I recall that I did my fair share of moaning too. It was a relief to be riding down the other side of "Carter Bar".

Exquisite, would describe the scenery on the far side of the border as buffeted by wind and rain. I hurtled downward, the road began to twist and turn and my Brakes I found were useless because of the rain, I found myself actually praying that I'd reach the bottom safely, I was leaning the Bike over on the bends as much as I dare. Slowly the brakes began to recover, and when I reached the bottom, I did the same. We slept soundly I might add at Jedburgh that night and returned home via the coast road the next day through another rainstorm. Today, each time I see a bicycle saddle I wince as I remember that trip to Jedburgh.

I was obliged to attend a course at night school just then, but I joined a Cooperative Youth Club in Benwell and had some great times there. Dances were held once a month and sometimes they were held at other CO-OP. branches. I well remember a special Dance held in the Coop hall at the top of Buckingham Street, near the big lamp on Westgate road. The theme of this affair was to be "What you wore when the ship went down so everyone was to dress accordingly, it was great fun looking around at friends, one dressed as a greaser, another in pajamas, a simply huge baby complete with pacifier and of course a Captain. Even a couple swathed in a blanket, I myself was a Waiter having borrowed my dad's tailed coat complete with a white cloth draped over my arm and a menu. Unhappily, I was so convincing that I was called to various tables all evening and told to dispense drinks at once. However, at the end of the evening the judges saw fit to bring me in "Second" so I had my time in the Sun.

The regular "Saturday night dance at Fawdon CO.OP. Hall was a certain favourite, we danced to Jack Phillips and his Band, Jack played the Hawaiian guitar and his friend Horsley Hall played Piano. When the interval arrived some of us would go up on stage and of course we'd request a favorite number or two for dancing. The band were always friendly and usually Jack would oblige. I have only recently learned that this man who was the mainstay of the music on those Saturday nights was a keen photographer and spent years recording scenes of the Newcastle he loved so well. I now have a book of his "Pictures of Newcastle" published by his son after Jack passed away in the 1980's.

When I was Seventeen my Dad took sick and was rushed to Hospital, it was his old Nemesis: the Stomach Ulcer, the Doctors Operated but could do nothing. Dad was brought home and passed away after a couple of weeks. The family fell apart, but, as families are wont to do, we picked up the pieces and as they say. Life goes on, But Just the same I felt his death was so untimely, words left unsaid, things not yet done, etc. I feel the pain, even today.

Summer time brought Club outings to Morpeth, Corbridge, Whitley Bay and the like. We went on week end Camping trips; Morpeth being the favourite, our usual Site was on the "Common", just behind the Grave Yard, needless to say, that even the occasional hoot of an Owl would set teeth chattering. Nobody could find the flashlight (of course). From time to time we boys had dates with the girls of the youth club much handholding, giggles and the like Ah Me! Where did the time go?

At nineteen I went to work for "Barney Berrry's", an Electrical shop in the city, a great bunch of guys including my dear friend Brian Reeves also from Pendower. As time went on I heard tales of high adventure and excitement from older guys when working away from home working on what was called "lodging jobs" One such electrician, Bob a real nice guy who worked at the same place told me that a friend of his, a foreman on a West Hartlepool job would take me on if I could start right away. This I did and I've never looked back.

I began to have dreams of owning my own transport; this led me to buying a 250cc motorbike it was an old "Raleigh", 1929 vintage, (Well! I had to start somewhere). This bike took me to and from work for quite a while; I even went to dances on it and the odd jaunt into the country on a Sunday. Like all things, it began to fall apart and so we said goodbye. About this time my brother Bobby was conscripted to do a spell in the Army and like many others he was not overly pleased by this, but he got on with it, and by and by of course he was "Demobbed". On his return to Newcastle, he and his young Lady made plans to be married; "Agnes" was her name a very pretty girl who lived just up the street from us.

A GEORDIE AT BAY

It was around 1950 I decided the time had come to try my hand at working on contracts away from home and moved my apprenticeship to Drake and Gorhams, said to be the oldest Electrical Contractors in England. It was exciting seeing different places and meeting tradesmen from all over the country. I worked for them at Workington in Cumberland, Consett at the Steelworks, Brampton, at a new high school where I officially "came out of my time" and became a journeyman Electrician ("look out world here I come"). I felt at the time that Consett was my "Waterloo". A new steel mill was to be installed, and I was part of a large crew of electricians and apprentices who traveled each day to this town by bus. I was in the final year off my apprenticeship with still much to learn and the new mill to be was in the forefront of technology.

The whole place seemed to be seething with humanity around the clock, I became lost more than once as I went back and forth between buildings. Working in front of the old furnaces was like being in Hell itself, as strange units, called chargers driven by an operator, brought up scrap metal and would race across the massive floor. Shaped rather like an army field gun with the operator sitting at the rear, and the huge scrap bucket fixed on the end of the " barrel." the whole contraption was suspended about two feet from the floor. At this point, one of the furnace doors would slide open and the scrap was disgorged into the belching flame causing an explosive roar to echo around the entire building although on looking around after each ear splitting occurrence everyone looked oblivious to it. After a while I guessed that I must have been the only one with shredded nerves. The scrap bucket was then withdrawn and the doors closed. These monsters hung from girders on tracks high above us and moving at high speed seemed to have regard for neither man nor beast. Moreover, while we were trying to repair some item in the middle of the huge floor in front of the ovens a yell would be heard "Look out" or "Hi Up" but the noise in that place was such that we kept a man on "lookout" the whole day. Even so, I prayed that I could leap out of the way fast enough.

At times, we would be sent into the "slab reheat" shop to install or repair a machine. This was the place where huge ingots of almost white-hot steel were set down on a conveyor. It was then run through massive rollers, which eventually reduced it to the width and thickness required at the time. An operator would shovel salt on it each time it headed for the roller press, this caused an ear shattering roar as shale was removed and scattered every where. These were no less than lethal missiles, usually shaped like broad swords and daggers; it scared the Heck out of me at the time. I kid you not. It was said that this process felled more than one man over the years.

I take my hat off to the steelworkers of this town who toiled as they did to bring wealth into the area and take care of their families. Of course, in those days despite the dangers, there was not even a hard hat between us. For a while, I traveled by motorbike to work, part of it during the winter, when even bus services were suspended because of extreme ice conditions. I can only suppose that some one was watching over me. No helmet, ill clad, I rode mainly one handed whilst banging one hand or the other against my thigh to restore circulation.

On my arrival, I was as stiff as a board and got many a jibe or a ribald comment from the guys about my appearance. One electrician never missed a chance to shout remarks about my bike and me. "How's that bag of hammers running today Jim?" He would say. Never mind I can only suppose he kicked the cat as he walked in his front door at night. I do hope he feels better now. If a project got behind schedule the crew would often be asked to "work a ghoster", this was the name given to working around the clock. It meant coming to work on say, Friday morning and leaving to go home on Saturday evening. It got to the stage when I hardly knew my own name. I was so tired. On the bus going back to Newcastle all of us dozing, heads nodding, we looked like a meeting of politicians. Middlesborough was next, Blackpool at the I.C.I. works, then Shotton Steelworks in North Wales, that would be 1954 I believe.

It was here that I teamed up with the Lad that I had known previously at Whickham view school, Denton Burn. Bill was also an Electrician. We had reasonable digs in Shotton, (as digs go that is) and as is common when away from home we worked much overtime and this way were able to save "a few Bob" for a rainy day. We met two guys in our digs who worked on the same job, Harry a cable Jointer from London and Pat his mate, Pat was an Irish man "of the first water" he was a delight to know and became a firm friend of mine. His sense of humour was very "Irish", I recall chiding him for coming in late one night, he just replied in his Irish brogue "Sure and one of these nights I'll be coming in so late I'll meet meself going out to work". I am afraid there is really no reply to that one.

Again, I digress, after some months Bill and I decided to make our presence felt in the "Smoke" (London). Whilst we were there we criss crossed London each day looking for work, we got to know the subway system and the big red buses as they bustled about, but it took a little time to finally land a job. There was the odd time that we took in a movie usually around the Edgeware Road in the afternoon or a couple of pints in the Kings Head. At last we took jobs with the "Express Dairies" who needed two Electricians for their Maintenance Department. Kilburn high street was where we took a room in a flat with a family above some shops.

As we stood there on our first day I knocked on the door and it was opened by the lady of the house, she was middle aged grey hair and a slight stoop and with a very kindly face. She told us that she did in fact have a vacant room and told us the charges. It was at about this moment that I noticed that she had a most peculiar habit of whistling between each statement she made, a few bars of various tunes, and (I gathered after a few minutes that she had quite a repertoire). It was almost impossible for Bill and I to refrain from giggling aloud so we spun around and scrutinized the passing traffic intently. Then gathering our wits we picked up our luggage and followed her indoors I noticed right away that there was a movie house and a launderette almost opposite our new digs. (Very practical I thought). It turned out that we were to make full use of them during our stay.

I do recall having a pillowcase full of my shirts socks and underwear etc ready for the wash one day but unknown to me our land lady, enterprising, and a wily old bird to boot, added some of her grand daughters "things" as well. The washing machine finished its cycle and I began to pull the clean clothes out and place them on a nearby table, it was then that I noticed some of the customers standing about were staring at some of the items; they were of course some very natty ladies underwear. Face burning I stuffed them into the pillowcase, and hastened out into the street.

Kilburn High Street was something to see on Saturday afternoon, an amazing variety of shops seething with people. I loved going to buy clothes there and besides I invariably met some of the guys and girls from the dance hall we frequented in Cricklewood.   After a while on our new job I came to realize that I was not liked by the Foreman of our work crew, he did not care for the way in which I was sometimes not quick enough to join the rest of the crew in standing at attention and crying out "good morning sir" as he entered the building. There came the day when his arrival coincided with me coming down a ladder carrying a fluorescent fixture that I had just removed. Observing the Company's safety rules I stored it in a safe place, however I was to discover that Ann Bolyn had nothing on me, and so ….Exit Jim.

At about this time my sister Sheila and her Fiancé, Alfie were going to be married in Newcastle so I packed a bag and went north. It was a tedious journey with stoppages every few miles because of an overheating engine. The railway system, by all reports was simply clapped out, owing to the effects of the recent war. Sheila's "husband to be" was also an electrician and a friend of mine, a canny lad, I'd worked with him from time to time around the area and they were going to live near the center of town. The reception was at the High Cross Co-op. Hall in Benwell, a favourite of local folks. It was on this occasion that I was reminded of my apparent resemblance to my late Father. Talking as I was to two friends, glass in hand in a corner of the room, a complete stranger walked up to me and cried out "you are your Dad's absolute double!" I've heard this said many times since.

I once again took a position with Drake and Gorham, this time with their London office; they sent a young South African lad from Durban, Brian Thorne and myself to Southampton to work with some people from their Winchester branch. It was at a girl's high school. We were there to install pyrotenax, (which is a copper sheathed cable) for some Sub Mains, as there was no one else trained to do it, so I was paid more than the local foreman. I was not terribly popular as you can imagine! Brian proved a good friend and when the job was complete, we were sent to another installation just outside of High Whickham, an ore plant, strangely enough, situated in the picturesque village of Chinnor just outside of High Whickham. Only a half dozen electricians on the job, the Foreman's name was Fred his Charge Hand was Wally, both from London Office. The whole crew on this job got on very well together and the work progressed accordingly, it lasted about five months as I remember.

We both had accommodation in a little cottage with a nice family, a lovely place, it looked like it belonged in a painting by "Constable," great food, feather beds but no indoor plumbing Oh well, you can't have everything as they say. We made many friends there, and of course enjoyed the local pubs. One of these establishments dated from the early seventeen hundreds, and had overhead beams which prevented most of the patrons from standing upright and the unwary would receive a crack on the head, (the folks in those far off days, I must suppose were much shorter in stature). the alternative was to go home with a crick in the neck. Still the beer was good and the folks were friendly. A monthly dance was held in the village hall and occasionally on Tuesday night a local bus would take us together with our girl friends to a picture house in the village of Princess Risborough, and usually we all had a good time. Of course, the job was duly completed and like ships that pass in the night, we parted. Quite sad!

Brian and I had one final night on the town, and parted company he was to sail back home to Durban and I headed for London to see my old friend Bill again. By this time he was staying with his Aunt, and Uncle who had an apartment in Sussex Gardens just off the Edgeware Road, and very kindly they let me stay there for a week or so. Bill and I had lots to talk about and we visited some of our old haunts, but Bill was now courting a young lady from Golders Green so I made my goodbyes and went home to visit Mam and my young sister in Newcastle.

My Sister at this time held a position with a Newcastle Shipping Company and in her spare time was active in Musical stage productions that came to the area. Her Holidays were most often spent with friends, hiking in various parts of the Continent.

After a stay at home, I began to feel the call of the wild once more. I went to Middlesborough, working this time at a chemical plant. A great crew of guys once again, hard work all day and usually out on the town at night, sometimes in Stockton, a market town only a bus ride away. On my way home to the digs in the evening I noticed a little car on a spare plot of land, an early 1930,s model, it never seemed to go anywhere, rain or shine there it was in the same spot. I sought out the owner who said he would take thirty pounds for it, Voila! My first car. All I needed now was driving lessons, and then my little "Morris 8"and me could go places.

Another friend of mine, Glen, living in Pendower phoned me; I mentioned earlier that he was a pal of mine since we were tots, he was a pipe fitter and said in a letter that he was at loose ends so, yes, you've guessed it, he arrived by the next train. Glen already held a driving license " so we had it made" (famous last words). We worked for a while in Middlesborough, but then after a while headed south to Leicester to work on the new extension of the John Lewis Partnership Store in the town centre, just half a dozen Electricians on this one, all about the same age as Glen and me. There were of course lots of girls in the store and we spent much of our time on dates in the evening, (as I said it was a nice *town*) The foreman was an older guy, about fifty I'd say and cantankerous with it. He was, to put it mildly, Something Else! So much so that we gave him a nickname; "The Scorpion," we felt it suited him, and believed that we were the only ones that thought so. We were somewhat taken aback when one morning the Building Contracts Manager himself walked up to us during tea break and asked "Is the Scorpion on site today?".

We prowled the dance halls in whatever town we were in. Glen, not wasting any time was soon dancing with a pretty girl and if I thought that he'd pipped me at the post I would take a girl dancing past him and In a stage whisper I'd say " Glen! Don't worry about it! Give it back to me when you get on your feet, wife and kids first now! Then having watched the girls jaw drop I'd scarper, rapid like! Before the night was over he would have his revenge of course perhaps telling a young lady that I was trying to impress "be careful Cos Jim here takes fits" the girl would gasp and I would wander off deflated. So much for friendly wickedness.

Working there was a lot of fun for us, but we all worked hard, and so they got their pound of flesh. We had decent digs again, which I'm sure the reader would agree is half the battle in a situation like ours. Our favourite watering place became the "Cherry Tree Pub"; we'd go there to meet our friends before going off together. Leicester people are very friendly and what was closer to my heart, there was a great dance hall. It was here that I met a girl named Christine, Blonde, Blue eyed, and vivacious. Much to my delight we hit it off from the start and began going out together. She was a great girl to be with and we quite often made a foursome with Glen and one of her friends. I seemed to get along with her family too; they owned a small Bakery in Leicester so we never went hungry. As I resumed traveling again my ties with Leicester began to slip away and once again "Ships That Pass in the Night" etc.

Glen and I spent some time in Cymbran, in Monmouthshire, on a new Electrical installation for the "Girlings" Brake Company. We didn't care for the job all that much but the area was very pretty; as were the twin sisters we met in the plant and promptly made a foursome. We made Pontypool one of our haunts and spent our free time with the girls, (Marjorie and Marion) going to movies or driving around the area, walks in the local park etc, We had quite a few friends there but we found the town of Newport very dull. (I nevertheless passed my driving test there). Their police, I found to be very understanding, we were stopped for speeding one night and I was able to explain that we'd just bought some fish and chips and we were hurrying home before they got too cold. I think the Constable was trying to refrain from laughing as he sent us off into the night.

Our next port of call, (if you will) that we headed for was Cleveleys just North of Blackpool, an I.C.I. Plant on a six-month job. Staying as we did with a family that ran a boarding house on the seafront, Glen and I were almost part of the family there; we became good friends with some young performers from the show on the north Pier. Every morning at breakfast they would be dressed in a different costume for their parts on stage with faces heavily made up and carrying props of various kinds. A weird scene wouldn't you say? Somehow breakfast didn't taste the same at the time, although it was all rather a giggle.

In a while we moved to some digs not far away: Doric house. On the main street, the lady's name there was Mrs. Wilding, she and her daughter shared the chores in the house and fed us very well. Her daughter was prone to practical jokes and it was not unknown for us to find a brick under the pillow or short sheets in the bed. On one occasion one of our guys who owned a Vesper motor scooter declared it was every bit as powerful as the car one of the other boarders owned. To prove this we must show four passengers on board the Vesper and in motion. And so it was that with one of us standing up as the driver, one on the rear seat, and one on the carrier, plus yours truly on the handlebars we did in fact proceed down Cleveleys promenade albeit very slowly. If nothing else it gave some evening strollers a chuckle.

When the job was finished at Cleveleys we did not wish to leave the area so we took on a short term job in Lytham, St. Annes just south of Blackpool. It was at the new Ministry of Agriculture Buildings built to house "Ernie" the Government Computer. During our stay in Blackpool area we made full use of the facilities thereabouts, and were duly introduced to the Tower Ballroom and The Winter garden. Money seemed to burn a hole in our pockets, we even hocked a watch and a couple of suits, at one point. You see "Joe Loss and his Band" were playing at the Tower, that evening and, well, first things first, don't you know? It was at a Tower dance that I met Freda, a blue eyed blonde, with a zest for living; she actually lived in Leicester, and like myself came to Blackpool where good wages were to be had.

Soon we were spending all our time together. We explored the town from end to end, took in most of the shows, Pubs and eateries. In so doing we saw many of the big stars in the various theatres and sometimes, in the street, literally. On turning a corner on the sea front one night and leaning into a strong wind, I stumbled into Tommy Trinder in company with Arthur Askey, (two famous English comedians). They were out for a stroll after their last show of the evening. As I left cigarette ash on his lapel, I quickly apologized but was told, "Not to worry". Standing at a bus stop one sunny afternoon, a bus drew up and Errol Flynn stepped off, (he didn't even say hello) never a dull moment! Our relationship although nourished by the famous Blackpool illuminations, ended on the last night of the season. Freda and I were in the last car lined up to tour the Lights, and as our wheels began to turn, the lights dimmed and went out. Just our luck! As a matter of fact much the same thing was happening to our friendship so Freda and I went our separate ways.

The Morris "8" ran like a charm for us but the miles were piling up and although she was well mannered she was rather small so Glen and I decided to get a bigger car and share the cost and so it was that we came into possession of a Vauxhall D.X. Model, 1936\37. I think, by our standards it was like a Rolls Royce.

After a while, we would get some time off and go up home to see the folks, and sample the local dances again. We danced many a night away at the Brighton Assembly rooms, Scotswood dance, Fenham dance and our great love, the Oxford Galleries situated in the city. George Evans the Bandleader and his rendering of my favourite song at the time" You Belong to Me" and so many others would charm everyone right to the Last Waltz I made many friends there, but just like always, we lose touch, although we swear we will not. I had the good fortune to ask a particular young lady for a dance one night, her name: Gladys and she lived in North Shields, very petite and pretty with dark hair and brown eyes we dated for some months and her impish sense of humour I can recall to this day.

During this time, I was working at the Steelworks at "Shotton," North Wales, a massive site, it even had its own bus service on the roads inside the walls of the. plant I came up to Newcastle for the new year celebrations and Gladys and I went to the "Milvain Dance" on the West Road, afterwards we went to a party at a friend's house, Lo and Behold most of our friends were already there. It being New Years Eve, we all partook of "Foody bits" with a "giggle and a drink" and a good time was had by all. I was with this lovely girl in and around Newcastle for the best part of a year and enjoyed every minute of it. I duly returned to the job at the steelworks and it was some weeks before I was able to get back to Newcastle. I found Gladys was not available, mainly my fault I guess, after all how many girls would want a vagabond for a partner? I only hope that life has been good to her.

As I write this story of mine, having met so many people, both friends and acquaintances, over the years, I realize that it has left a gallery of moving pictures in my mind for me to look at and remember. At night as I lie in bed and the lights are low, I at times call them up. To the People I have failed to mention in this story I would like to say that, as one gets older, ones memory is not as good as it was etc, but by now you probably all realize that anyway. Nevertheless to you I apologize.

One fateful day Glen and I took a job with a contractor at the Vauxhall motor plant in Luton Bedfordshire. It was a huge sprawling site with umpteen contractors working there, a building that would turn out the brand new 1957 "Vauxhall Victor" Glen took a room for himself in Luton while I myself looked at some ads in the window of a newsagent for digs, seeing none there I went inside to enquire. A lady customer overheard what I said and promptly told me that she was looking for "a nice young man" to live with her family and herself. Why on earth was she looking at me? I hear you ask) and so it was that I went to live in "Round Green" outside Luton the reason being that I preferred to have meals, laundry etc as well as a room. They were a Great family Mr. and Mrs. Pettit and their daughter Eileen, lovely digs, lovely people. Mr. Pettit worked on the assembly line at the Vauxhall plant and when I saw him at work _ he worked very hard and was _ always bathed in sweat, never the less his love for his family stood out like a beacon. All his spare time was spent on his house renovating it inside and out. Whenever I returned from work, I'd find him up a ladder painting or bustling around moving furniture. With a cheerful "hello Jimmy", he would stop what he was doing to have a cup of tea with me. I always will remember him as one of nature's gentlemen. I moved away after a while although we did exchange a letter or two, then tragedy struck, he got very sick and died. I regret to say that I lost touch with his family after a while.

By now I had a little 10 hp. "Standard" car square body, coach built, very nice, I always thought her engine sounded like an "Armstrong Siddeley", which as you car buffs may know was rather a posh car produced in the 1930's, and was famous for its very sweet whine from the engine. The draw back with regards to having a car in England, at least at that time, was that should you leave your car over night without lights it meant a ticket and a fine, and I got a number of them. It cost a fortune! Silly law I thought, even then.

Glen and I drove to a dance in Hitchin one night, a town not too far from Luton, it was held in what was known as the "Hermitage hall" and it was here that I met Sheila my wife. I approached this young lady and asked "Could I have this dance please?" The rest is History, and I consider myself a very lucky man. We began going steady, tootling around the countryside, dances, movies, walks etc. The first movie that we saw together was "The King and I" at a Theatre in Hitchin. On some weekends Sheila would take me to "Walkern", a village just outside Stevenage to visit her Aunt Sis, Uncle Son and their children Erika and Peter, they had a Smallholding just outside the village.

It was here that Sheila took up permanent residence after a while. I would go calling on her up there and was always made more than welcome; we all got on so very well that there came a time when I thought of them as my own family. Uncle Son was a man I took to right away, he was well read and we would often sit around in the evening swapping yarns and discussing World affairs. It was obvious to me that by Uncle Sons every word and deed that he loved his family very much. Aunt Sis, Erica and Peter were fun to be around, forever quoting something from "the Goon show", which was our favourite Radio Program. I was even asked to spend a Christmas with them at Walkern and will always treasure the memory of that time.

I decided that I should look for a different car and with that in mind; Sheila and I began looking at various used car lots. It was in "Round Green" we found a "Morris 8 Series E" at "Stevenson's Garage", it was a nice balmy summers evening and the chap there suggested we take it for a drive. The three of us climbed aboard and I drove, we got as far as Hitchin where we stopped at a little Pub for a "jar", very acceptable. I picked up the car the following day.

I got word from Newcastle that my Mam had passed away suddenly, and I should go home at once. I was in my car heading North within 20 minutes, A journey I can hardly recall. Before I knew it, I was in Newcastle and I was there about two weeks or so. The Funeral took place, and what few possessions Mam had were sold off, a sad end to the Story of "My Parents". I considered trying to keep the Council house on, thereby giving Margaret and I a Home, but the local Council office in the City said:" as the Head of the house has gone, we must leave". (After all my Family had only spent thirty years paying them rent) "Long Life to all Council Members" May their Deeds hang around their necks as they tread the Red Hot Coals. I then returned south, and my Sister Margaret went to live in digs with friends.

I now had digs in Luton at Newcombe Road with a Mr. and Mrs. Hunt an older couple, there was as many as ten or so men staying there at any one time. The house was large enough of course but I wondered how she managed. She cooked lovely meals for every one, did all the washing and had to do her own shopping too, she even had a half dozen cats and a sweet disposition "don't fiddle arse about in my kitchen" she would say laughingly to me if I was in her way. Mr. Hunt was a fine old person, he did Insurance work part time, but I think I'll always remember him pottering about the house winding up the various clocks (and there were many) or sitting at the table repairing them, always a smile, always a joke. They were, I'm sure you can tell, devoted to each other.

I think it only right and fair to mention at this point the army of landladies I have known in England. Many and varied would be the correct term, from hard working to otherwise so to speak. Mostly with their children grown up and married they quite often showered young men like me with motherly love, to fill a gap I suppose.

These care givers had to be early risers each day and at times the weekends also. Being young we would often be out at night on the town, coming in at a late hour we would usually find a welcome snack waiting for us on the table. And so dear ladies I pause to salute you all wherever you may be, for making life just a bit more bearable than it might have been.

During that same period Glen was stopped in his tracks, he met, and fell for a young lady from "Houghton Regis", a village just outside Dunstable her name was Joyce, and what a lovely girl she was. As a foursome, we went all over together, became firm friends of the family and were invited to many parties at the house. In a matter of months, they decided to get married and Glen took a job in the maintenance department at the Vauxhall Motors Plant in Luton.

THE WHITE MAN'S GRAVE

I began to think after a while that I would like to see something of Africa before I "settled down," (I'd been told by all and sundry that "Wanderlust" is what happens to a young lad).

I had an interview at "Barlowe and Young" (Electrical Contractors) in Victoria, London it seems they wanted an Electrical Supervisor to go out to West Africa right away, I spoke with the Director, an ex Navy man who said to me "Look here, I like the cut of your Jib ("Good Heavens!") And after selling my car, I spent my last evening with Sheila, packed my bags, and off I went.

It was freezing cold at London Airport, and this was to be my very first flight, accordingly I acted very casual, as though I circumnavigated the Globe every other day, (I suspect that only half of the passengers saw through my clever posturing). It was quite a severe Winter, with Ice and snow everywhere, Then the flight was delayed, they told us it was necessary to pre heat the engines in the hanger, (it was one week prior to this that an aircraft crashed in Germany killing most of the Manchester United Soccer team) I wasn't nervous, I tell you! Hell No! That knocking` sound was only my knees giving vent to their feelings. They took us on a bus across to the other end of the airport and into the hanger, and there she stood, a Boeing "Stratocruiser, developed from the airframe of the famous Boeing B29 Super Fortress. Very impressive.

I had a first class ticket, a comfortable seat, excellent food and great service, a British airline, BOAC (of course). I have flown many miles since on various airlines and I have never seen the like again. We stopped to refuel in Rome and then on to Kano in Northern

Nigeria, here a few of us disembarked. As I walked away from the aircraft it came to me that I was truly in a different world, the intense heat after the freezing cold in England was the first reminder.

As I walked to the customs building it seemed that I was almost tripping over small lizards that were scampering everywhere, about 12 inches long, the females slightly shorter a bright green head with a light brown body, the male an orange head and a scaly dark blue body. All the while, running and abruptly changing direction they would do what I called "a couple of push ups" whenever they stopped. I learned that it was to increase their visible horizon. I stayed at the "Rest House" along with two other passengers, a Scotsman and an Irishman although they were "Three Sheets to the wind" during the flight from UK, and did not recall any of it the following morning. They were frisky to say the least, and were mortified as I told them that they had demanded a hug from the stewardess. These two were what was known in the vernacular as "old Coasters". They were on their way back from leave to the new wharf facility at Port Harcourt. When I was at a loose end I was often asked over to their club dance and to meet some other guys. While we were together they filled me in on much of what I should know as a newcomer to what was known as the "White mans grave" (Charming!).

They took me on a tour of Kano, when we first got off the plane including a visit to the huge Market. It is said that a person can purchase any thing there and when we finished walking, I believed them. I remember thinking that I should like to buy a snake skin, and was shown to where a man sat in the middle of a circle of large baskets, which contained live snakes; he declared that he had just the right one for me. I almost jumped out of *my* skin as he plunged his hand into one of the baskets and slowly hauled out the biggest snake I've ever seen in my life. He then pried its jaws open, thrust his foot right down its throat and commenced to remove the head with a large carving knife moving it around the neck in one neat movement, leaving the huge body threshing on the ground. I slunk away but not before leaving him the money for his trouble. Brave white hunter! (who *said that?*) It was about this moment when I recalled a play that I had heard on BBC Radio called "Shopping, lovely Shopping".

I was up early next day and for the first time I watched the majesty of an African Sunrise. A Dc3. Aircraft took me to Port Harcourt in Eastern Nigeria where I was to do the Electrical Installation at a new Showroom for "Lever Bros," the soap company. The heat was intense, as I have said the humidity very high and insects of all kinds plentiful. Africa meets a person as soon as the door of the aircraft is opened; it's rather like stepping into an oven accompanied by that unique earthy sweet\sour smell that only Africa can produce.

It was a great experience nevertheless, and being young and Daft as they say, I soldiered on. I found that the installations I was to be concerned with were to be all in Pyrotenax cable and as nobody here had yet even seen the

stuff let alone work with it. I realized as soon as I arrived that I'd need help. A young man came seeking work, his name was Emanuel Okeke, and He lived in this region, and was of the Ibo tribe. I'm pleased to relate that by time I was ready to leave for England, Emanuel was very proficient in this type of work. Of all the things I did in West Africa, employing Emanuel was the best decision I made. We got on so well from the start; cheerful, hard working and he always looked out for me wherever we went. Emanuel was an educated lad and spoke English very well but I myself ran into difficulty when trying to get a point across to some of the people who had spent most of their life out in the Bush.

The very first European men to come "to the coast" as traders were the Portuguese and they found difficulty in making themselves understood to the local people and so they devised what is now known as *pidgin English*, I boned up on this and it served me well during my sojourn in this country. I would further claim that without it's use the country would never have had a successful self government. Imagine that to ask a person to go from point a. to point b. it would be "makee go dere for here." In answer to a question on the progress on a given job, it might be "please sir it remains small" or on enquiring as to whether a particular person was in the building you might be told "he is not on seat". Similarly, getting home one night and being tired I asked my steward to "pass chop". (food) Oops! The one I liked the most was, when retiring for the night, turn to your friends and say simply, "unless Tomorrow!"

On Saturday lunch time a lot of expatriates went to eat at the rest house, so called as it had accommodation like a hotel and of course a large dining area. On the menu the main course was always curried chicken, a great favourite, and not for the faint hearted. (as I was to learn) After a few beers we would order this delicious repast and the meal would begin. It consisted of chicken stew cooked in a curried sauce with side dishes of various fruits and nuts fried as well as plain. It was at this time that I did the inevitable. I scooped up a generous portion of peppers from my plate and began to eat them. I was so busy talking that I realized too late what I had done, It left me gasping, and it took at least three ice cold beers to assuage that fiery explosion in my mouth. I vowed "never again," (The peppers that is).

When Sunday came around we three younger lads were usually at a loose end, so after spending some time writing letters home We'd leave Len to have his weekly afternoon snooze while we would drive off into the bush and seek out local sights taking a picnic with us. On one such occasion we decided to go to a branch of the Niger river to look for Crocodiles. Not even a fishing net between us. Ah, foolish youth! Being told by some local village folks that crocs went deep to avoid the heat of the day, we resorted to using long branches from a tree to convince them to rise but to no avail. Walking a few feet away from the bank to get a longer pole for myself I chanced to look back at my friends and saw to my horror that on a tree branch overhanging the head of one of them was a mean looking green snake, it looked as if it was poised to strike. Seeing the danger I called him to come over to me right away as I'd found something in the grass that he should see, he did then I pointed out the snake. He said he was relieved that I had the presence of mind to call him over as I did, more so when we were told that this snake would spit at it's intended victim always striking the eyes. Never a dull moment so they say!

It was a matter of adjusting to the West African way of life. Such things as having an electric lamp always burning on the floor of the wardrobe to fight high humidity which creates mildew and destroys shoes and clothes Filter all drinking water and keep away from snakes of course. Termites were also a curse in this part of the world, and I was told by a friend of mine that one day he merely leaned against the front door frame where he lived and the whole thing collapsed in a cloud of dust. (And don't forget your daily anti- malarial medication).

I was advised by old Coasters at times to always take care to include plenty salt in my diet, and I learned the hard way. I'd been staying with a couple of guys who gave me a room at their place while I was working in Port Harcourt and was on my way to the job site in the Morris Minor, a typical hot dusty morning. My eyes for some reason began to ache quite suddenly and developed into a blinding headache, as I arrived at my place of work. I stopped the car and with great difficulty struggled to stand up.

After resting against the car I lurched inside and tried to speak to Emanuel But his voice seemed to be garbled and quite far away. The return journey to my room was very much like a nightmare of the first water as I swerved about the road quite a lot and on my arrival I just fell on the bed and past out. Some hours later my friend showed up and helped me to sit up in the bed made some tea, and then to my surprise ordered me to taste the perspiration on the back of my hand. I did so and found it lacked salt, he then made me a sandwich of salt smeared thickly onto the butter in it, then stood over me while I bit into it. I slept the rest of the day and woke up at teatime feeling as they say, like a two year old. (lesson learned).

One aspect of West Africa that fascinated me was it's Insects, from the Flying Ants to the huge Rhino Beetles. One evening I was sitting by a single lamp reading a book, a spooky one about vampires etc. Quite suddenly, a shadow passed by me into the gloom on the far side of the room. To say I got a fright would be an understatement, but I recovered and went to investigate and found a Moth on the wall with a wingspan of *no less than nine inches,* "Welcome to Africa Jim".

On a Saturday I would often go into town to do a little shopping for myself, a book or two, toiletries and if I was lucky UK newspapers, although they would be at least a month old, nevertheless, most welcome. It was on such an excursion such as this that I discovered that a particular store offered facilities to customers wishing to send audio tapes instead of letters to friends or loved ones far away. I availed myself of this on occasion. Of course I did not know it then but it turned out to be my introduction to a medium that I was to be involved with for years to come. I would have the same name for my business in California as that of the store in far away West Africa: "Kingsway"!

The only place to go for entertainment and to meet other English people was the European club in Port Harcourt; it was quite large and had a few hundred members and some wives. I'd see an outdoor Movie there (It's the only place I've seen a lizard crawling around on a film stars face) Then I'd have a couple of beers and a yarn with some lads from U.K. doing the same sort of work that I was doing. A dance was held once a month and that was very popular, as well as Bingo Sessions etc.

My company informed me after a while that when I had finished the showroom and warehouse, I was to go to "Aba", 40 miles inland to complete a contract at a large "Unilever" soap plant. The work was already in progress and the man in charge of the Installation was Len, a senior foreman from London.   I'd met Len on my arrival and he'd shown me around It was arranged that I spend three weeks with him in Aba, going over the work to be done. The Company needed him for yet another Contract, this time in Jamaica. The house that Len had rented and lived in was now mine to use along with a very nice car (a Morris Traveler) and of course the equipment needed to finish the job.

During my time with Len he told me many tales of the skullduggery of the servants at the house, the one that really made me chuckle was about Lens mosquito boots. Len rarely wore these boots but humidity was so high in that part of the world that he had them regularly polished and they were kept standing on the floor in the living room by the sideboard. Each day after work, having had his tea he would make notes on the progress on site, and write sundry letters etc. One day as he sat there he noted that the boots were now situated at the other end of the sideboard. Thinking that perhaps the steward had moved them to facilitate sweeping the room, he went to bed. The following days showed the boots to be in various other places until finally they stood by the back door. Len, arriving home from work that day, and looking to see where the boots might be, (but in the house they were not) he thought to him self "the game's afoot"! (Pun intended!) as they were nowhere to be seen. Of course, there was much palaver, denials, pleadings but all was resolved because the boots were found outside the front door the following day. It seems that the miscreant had second thoughts. (Ahem!), or perhaps the boots had just gone for a stroll! (Egad! sir! A play on words!) It was not long before Len was packing his cases then I saw him off on the plane.

Down a hill outside of Aba was a river from where water was to be pumped to serve the soap works. A pump house was sited on the side of the hill with a narrow footpath leading down and it was to this place I went to begin to complete the remaining electrical installation. It was also I might add, the place where I encountered soldier ants for the first time, (I think I still carry the scars). I did the work there very quickly and scarpered.

I was on that Job about three months and wherever I went I could hear the talking Drums, from a village down by the river which had drums playing just about every day and could send messages using a relay system, a hundred miles in just a couple of hours. These incessant drumbeats covered any Departures, arrivals, births and deaths in the area. (I wouldn't mind, but I don't speak a word of the language) I'm afraid that it does get to you at times. Stories abound of District officers being driven mildly crazy over the years as they sat alone in their "Gida" (dwelling) well into the night.

After about three months, when both projects were complete I packed up and headed back to U.K. and Sheila. I thought I had seen the last of Africa. It was at this point that the company told me that I'd be needed on a Project in Kingston Jamaica when I returned to the UK. Unfortunately it never did materialize so once again I headed for London and Sheila.

Once I was at home again Sheila and I realized that we were in need of a car and after looking around, we bought a used "Ford Popular" a sort of beige colour, nothing to write home about I might add, very Spartan, didn't even have turn signals. So I installed some myself, it nevertheless showed itself to be a hardy vehicle.

Sheila and I decided to take the plunge and we were married in a little church in Walkern, which is a village just outside Stevenage. A few days before the great event we went to visit the minister who was to hold the ceremony and he had a little chat with us about married life and so on. He told me in particular that to love, honour and "obey" did not mean the I should tell my wife (for instance) "bring me my boots", it was rather that I should have the final word on things such as which colour the house should be painted or the type of car we should buy. Each of us should have input on the decision. (I guess I must have looked the dark or broody kind to him). However, "fair comment", I've always thought.

It was a small Wedding, attended by our close friends Glen and Joyce. Mr. and Mrs. Pettit came and Eileen, Sheila's Dad of course, her brothers and all her grandparents were there. We had a reception at aunty Sis's and as we didn't have much money we bought a used caravan to live in. Made by a company called Thompson an eighteen footer and very well made.   We bought it used from a couple In Stevenage who I might add were very sorry to see it go. We put it on a site next to Whipsnade Zoo, not the best choice I guess, but after a while we just tuned out the growls and the howling at night. Sheila was quite nervous at first, I myself was not perturbed, and still, that may have been because I was on Night shift at "Vauxhall Motors" in Luton at the time. (Joke!).

Glen and Joyce were living in their own Caravan right next to us and had been there for some time, so they showed us the ropes. The job at "Vauxhall Motors" maintenance department was a good decision as I realized that now I was married it would not make sense to travel away on contracts. We bought a wooden shed to put next to our caravan, it arrived in pieces and Sheila and I promptly put it together, (Talk about Laurel and Hardy!) I installed a bench with a vise on it (although mind you, Sheila did tell me that I had enough "vices" to begin with. (But lets not get into that!)

I remember getting all enthused about our new home, I dug a soak away pit for "gray water" from our trailer as there was no drainage system on site (very primitive) one week end I put a wooden fence all around our little home, complete with garden gate. Then as there was no electricity on site I installed a small generator, bolted it down next to the shed, and even made a muffler to suppress the noise. Looking back, Sheila and I agree that we must have looked like a couple of kids playing "House", but after all is said and done, that's what we were doing I suppose. Do I sound domesticated? Well it happens to the best of us I'm told, and I was enjoying it. Sheila was a hard working girl and a good wife, Her Cooking was terrific, still is! Saturday was usually shopping day in Luton and or Dunstable, after this we would go to the local baths to attend to our Ablutions. It was a toss up which one of us looked more like a lobster when we came out. Then lunch at Merryweathers our favourite Luton café, and perhaps take in a local movie.

After about a year I got the yen to go to West Africa again. Sheila came with me when I went for the interview. It was a company called "Agar Cross" in London; they needed a Supervisor for a subsidiary of theirs in Lagos, Nigeria, called "West African Engineering". She waited in the outer office for me, and after a short while I came out beaming, I had the job.   She smiled when I told her, but looked a little forlorn when I said she couldn't come with me. After a few seconds had passed I added, "you'll have to wait a little while, and then follow me out", I would not have even considered the job unless she was to be with me.   We celebrated with a meal at Lyons teashop in "Victoria". (The original big spender?) Sheila arranged to stay with Aunty Sis and Uncle Son at Walkern. While I was away I knew that the Company would be in touch to arrange her flight to join me. As I had to leave quickly we had the caravan towed up to Walkern where Uncle Son promised to take care of it, he even let me leave my "Ford Popular" in his yard.

In a few days I was in Lagos, it is a city on an Island Linked as it is to the mainland by "Carter Bridge". This city seethes with humanity from early morning until late at night. Ikoyi was another island nearby. It also boasts a bridge to the mainland but it used to be reached by paying a ferryman five cowrie shells, (the local currency then) to cross the water. Today it is still known as Five-Cowrie creek. In the office, I met Bert Bampton, my boss, who told me that I was supposed to begin the work on the new Bristol Hotel in the City centre. However, as the foundations were not even complete, I was to go up North to do an installation at a new boy's college in "Keffi" just over 700 miles into the Bush. We loaded up two "Opel Kapitan" station wagons with enough gear to start the job and with Bert driving one of the vehicles we headed north.

We went through village after village, town after town, each vehicle creating its own dust storm, and oh! The names as we sped by, Abeokuta . . Ibadan . . Ogbomosho, Ilorin . . Jebba . . Even as I write, the scenes are still vivid in my mind, Women, usually carrying something on their heads, walking along, perhaps to Market. The children were playing . . waving when they saw us, and crying out the usual "Omegu Onyosha" ("give money White man"). So I replied saying Omegu Enuji. (Give money Black man)" (A little humour there"). The oppressive heat and dust was ever present . No air conditioning in those cars I'm afraid.

We saw much impressive scenery as we journeyed north and at one point had to stop the vehicles to allow a gang of Baboons, (or is it a flock? Joke!) To cross the road, of course we thought it prudent to stay well back as they had young'uns with them, but they gave us the "once over" as they ambled along

anyway. As we pulled away I looked to my right. About 50yards from the roadside by some fallen trees at the edge of the Forest were numerous pairs of eyes looking our way.

We stayed the night in "Bida" at a Government Rest House and pressed on the following day through "Abuja" arriving at Keffi at about teatime. The local District Officer, (D.O). a Welshman by the name of Glyn, arranged that I could have a small Bush Rest House to live in. We looked over the job Site then had dinner at the Main Rest house and sat talking to Glyn under what proved to be the only ceiling fan for miles around. He related to us that that I'd arrived just in time for the "Rainy Season" which he took care to tell me always increased the snake population" OH JOY! Bert returned home to Lagos the next day.

One day soon after I arrived I had a pleasant surprise, my friend, Emanuel from Port Harcourt days knocked on my door and said he wanted to work for me again, I'd written to him from Lagos and he simply jumped on a train and headed North. My lucky day!

I now needed a cook\steward so I put the word out in the village, after a day or so an old man knocked on my door and said he would like the job. Slight of stature, robed, with aquiline features, he said he was of the Hausa tribe and lived in Keffi. His papers told me he'd been with his last employer 31 years; (Just as I thought; a quitter) A man and wife; Mr. and Mrs. Topercary who worked for the Forestry Commission. "Hassan" was an elder of the village of Keffi, and as such, was much

respected. As we got to know each other better he told me much of his life with these people and how he went on treks for weeks on end. Horses were the usual transport and in rough country, it was by foot. The river Niger was also their highway. Many times in very large canoes rented from villages along the way with kru boys, experts on the river to operate them. Plus a couple of baggage handlers He also told me that as there were few medicines in those far off days they carried cases of whiskey to ward off Malaria (I wish I'd thought of that). Hassan and I got along famously from day one, and he proved to be a mine of information. It was usual for a person to give a steward ten shilling every other day to cover groceries and incidentals and this is what I did. One morning I asked what I could expect for Dinner in the evening and was told Chicken.

After work, I came home and was told by Hassan that he needed one more Shilling to cover purchases. I went to the back door safe in the knowledge that chickens were commonly one shilling apiece, and gazing at the birds running around I just knew that he was on the fiddle I asked him which one of these "birds" is so big that it cost eleven shillings. Hassan looked at me puzzled for a moment then said, "Please sir," All! Not to be outdone "I asked shouldn't it be in the refrigerator?" "I got very good price on twelve of them, I keep them outside, feed them small, leave plenty room in refrigerator"… "Here Endeth the Lesson!"

Hassan's kitchen was separate from the house situated at the back about twelve feet beyond the back door. Brick built, about ten feet long by six feet wide and very primitive. It contained two empty five gallon kerosene cans lying on their sides about four feet apart. These were the ovens. The stove top consisted of some stout steel mesh lying across the two cans; the fire place of course was in between them. Not for Hassan the chopping of wood, he would use a ten or fifteen foot branch from a tree, putting one end in the fireplace, then set it on fire and the other end protruding through the open doorway, (less work for him he said). At times I'd come home and see black smoke billowing out obscuring the interior, including Hassan, he'd emerge to tell me about the meal he was preparing and to push the burning log a little further in when needed. I was always incredulous on seeing the great meals he produced.

Half a dozen Electricians arrived by train from Lagos and I employed some local lads to help out, and so the work began. The one thing I needed was the "Linesman's tackle" to pull in the overhead cables, but it never came

68

and so I resorted to using the car to pull them in. Passing a cable through successive insulators, and then securing it to the front bumper of the car I slowly reversed the vehicle, all the while watching the suspended cables until it reached the estimated amount of "sag", according to current specifications My next move was to run across to a point about ninety degrees to the cable run to see if the "sag" was now correct, before leaving the car to do this a log was placed in front of the wheels to hold it in place and off I'd run. Soon the overheads were complete but not before I'd almost burned out the clutch, also in stepping back to view my work I twice trod on an Anthill, much to the amusement of the local farm workers (ouch!)

I got along well with half a dozen Teachers who were also from England; we'd find reasons galore to get together for "Dwinky's" or "Din, Dins". One chap from the college was Tony Blair, an agricultural expert, he was working with local farmers to improve their crops which suffered mightily from all the pestilence that West Africa had to offer, they had great respect for this man and always referred to him in their language as " Sarkin Goana", (King Gardener).

Not long after I arrived in Keffi, Tony brought his Fiancé (Selma) out from England (she was *also* a Geordie Bless her!) and they were married in "Jos", a town about 150 miles to the North East situated high up on a plateau. All Tony's friends traveled up from Keffi to the reception, a tortuous road, but well worth it for the climate: misty mornings and very cool evenings, a nice change from Keffi with 100 degrees plus, and 99% humidity. Of course, our bread and butter was in Keffi, so after a couple of days we headed on back there. I remember being very grateful that the car behaved very well on the trip back being warned it was very dangerous to stop for very long on such a road we stopped only briefly for a sandwich and to view the very impressive scenery.

I invited Tony and Selma over for lunch one Saturday and Hassan served us a great curried chicken with all the trimmings, he even had an orchid which he presented to Selma with great ceremony. Selma was really touched, I was so impressed and told him so. The lunch was very well received though I kidded him saying that he should do it every lunch time.

We considered ourselves very fortunate at Keffi in that we had electricity from six o'clock until eleven each evening, supplied from a small generator at the College. It was really a boon to me as I read books a great deal at night. It was there that I developed the habit of having more than one book "going" all the time, Westerns, Who Dun-its, War stories and so on. Time did hang heavy on my hands, that's one reason why we worked on site at weekends.

I was obliged to drive to "Gudi", the rail junction about twice a week to see if any supplies had arrived, a distance of thirty eight miles, often without seeing another vehicle only to return to Keffi empty handed. The nearest telephone was at Gudi and was connected to Lagos only two days of the week, but I never did manage to "get through".

It was a common occurrence on the African roads to see vehicles overturned or in a ditch, I've even seen a Volkswagen up a tree (don't ask). On one trip to Gudi, Emanuel and I came across a "Mobil" Petrol Tanker lying on its side, Petrol leaking merrily out of the ports on the top into the ditch at the roadside. It should be noted that truck drivers over there were, what shall I say? A wild bunch! Yes, I think that is what I would say. Accidents on the road were commonplace, but what made it so difficult for the police was that the driver concerned usually jumps out of the vehicle after a mishap and disappears into the "bush". On inspection of the aforementioned leaking petrol tanker we found that the leaves of the rear springs were tied together with *string*, unbelievable, but true! So, I took a picture of it.

I recall that on one lonely trip back to Keffi I espied a Chameleon walking across the road in front of the car. In need of a diversion anyway, I stopped the vehicle and observed the leisurely progress of this little fellow as he slowly placed one foot carefully in front of another. Of course it was the least traveled road I'd seen in a long while, and so it was perhaps unlikely at his slow gait he would have a tragic encounter with a vehicle even so I marveled at his good fortune thus far. I decided that as he and I were fellow travelers so to speak, I should lend him a hand, I stooped and picked him up, placing him safely on the side of the road as, eyes rolling around and mouth agape he hissed roundly at me. I walked away admonishing him loudly for taking such risks etc. As I got back into the car I was relieved to see that there were no witnesses to this encounter.

It was on one of these forays into the countryside that I came across two young "Pagan" girls, each carrying a calabash on their heads, with bows and arrows slung over their shoulders. My partner on this trip was Joseph, a young Lagos man. We had taken a break from the long arduous drive, and pulled off to the side of the dirt road. We were both sitting in the car, sipping a Fanta orange drink when they approached. I smiled at them, greeting them in the Hausa language and offered one of them my bottle. By this time, Joseph was hysterical… crouching in his seat, gabbling that they would surely kill us both. Actually, the girls were giggling and pointing at me and asking for money. One of them accepted the drink, but to my dismay, upended the bottle and poured it onto the ground. I think they drank only water, and saw little value in the colored drink, or perhaps they thought it dangerous. Maybe they perceived the clear glass bottle being more valuable as a container. I then told Joseph to act friendly by smiling, which he did. I was glad because he was making the girls nervous, and I had heard that these people were very proficient with their weapons. It was told to me that in this society the females were the breadwinners whilst the men could usually be found sitting around the camp fires in the village telling stories. On giving the other bottle to them, they again asked for money. I asked in "Hausa" if I could pay them money in exchange for a photograph of me with them ("Change-y!   Change-y!"). As I watched them walk away from us down the road holding hands, quite

naked, swinging the soda bottles, I realized that these people would never drink a white man's concoction, it *was* the bottle that they valued. I think there's a lesson in this somewhere.

Every so often, I would go to "Kaduna", the nearest town, (200 miles of very bad laterite Road) to buy tobacco, soap, and Sweets and the usual three week old newspapers from U.K. Passing through many villages on the way I was made aware of the ever present Vultures, whilst being as ugly as sin, but protected by law these scavengers swaggered about the market place chasing away anything or anybody that looked as though they might be interested in any goodies that they laid had claim to. On an early trip, one of these birds took my car as a threat and died because of it. Mind you, they are graceful in flight, having a wingspan of 5/10 feet but my favorite company, they are not.

On an earlier trip I bought a "Grundig" tape recorder and some music tapes, many were the nights that the voices of Nat King Cole, Dean Martin, Bing Crosby and many more Stars could be heard floating across the African Bush from my little house. I found that invitations to dinner were suddenly on the increase, but it was usually joined by "Oh Jim! don't forget to bring your tape recorder" and your music tapes. I often wonder how many dinners I'd have missed if I had not owned a tape recorder. I could have starved to death! I still have that Music Mix today, and its always been referred to as "Keffi Music".

It was this same recorder that one night began to issue forth a strange squealing noise, and being of a curious nature, I opened it up. The sight that met my eyes showed to my chagrin it was in fact an old and very much used machine. Recognizing that I had been taken for a "Charley" so to speak. I was back In Kaduna the following weekend.   The Lebanese owner was at his counter as I carried in the defective merchandise. To avoid the palaver that I knew would ensue, I explained that in the confusion of the day he'd apparently given me a machine that was "not new", this being so I needed a replacement "Pronto" he was extremely apologetic (groveling is a better word) and carried a brand new one out to the car.

At night in Keffi the sounds that Africa conjured up were many, varied and at times frightening, however I was usually preoccupied with visits of nocturnal creatures *inside* the house. As a matter of habit I always had a flashlight and a pair of sturdy slippers, with me under the mosquito net, these were needed if I went to the bathroom, aside from mosquitoes the footwear helped when I put my foot to the floor and heard large black scorpions scurrying for cover, these creatures measured as much as six inches in length.

At times, I would have an "insect evening". Leaving only one wall light on I'd sit in the darkest part of the room and watch as flying ants swarmed in through the open door. They would go straight for the light and within a minute or so it was impossible to see across the room, filled as it was with a horde of flying ants. One after the other they would drop to the floor and eject their wings Mother Nature apparently commands them to seek for a new nest. It is now that the little Gecko lizard comes for dinner, a translucent creature that makes his home in nooks and crannies inside the house and keeps the insect population at bay. Dashing across the floor, he'll grab an ant and make short work of it, then on to the next one. After a while his movements slow down until he can eat no more then he crawls away to sleep it off, leaving his accomplices to continue the feast. All this while a Praying Mantis sitting on the edge of the doorframe reaches out, snatches at an ant in flight, and begins to leisurely eat it alive, neatly biting the wings off as it does so. Lastly, come some immense frogs, as many as a dozen jumping noisily along the garden path to the doorway "to clean up." Only a few ant stragglers escape the slaughter but it is nature's way to maintain the food chain and who am I to argue? The only thing remaining is to sweep away the thick carpet of wings left by the marauders. It was in Keffi that I was told of an expatriate who sent a dead praying Mantis home to his wife in the UK and wrote " look at the size of mosquitoes out here" mind you, after seeing some of the huge sores on some of the local people and the sickness it brings I don't think I'd be so surprised.

The three seasons in West Africa are the hot (or dry) season, the wet season and the "Harmattan" (this translated means the "The wind of the White Horsemen.") it blows sand off the Sahara across the whole country and covers everything with a fine layer of the stuff. It gets into food of course, creates red-rimmed eyes, sore lips and general misery all around; I understand it has been known to get as far as the south of England.

The rain in this country is heavy and there's lots of it, together with lightning, which sometimes rolls sparkling in sheets across the grassland, that plus an increase in the snake population and more than the usual amount of mosquitoes at night. (Dear reader, I hope I haven't turned you off your vacation plans). It was on such a night as this, with all other Europeans out of the area (or so I thought) I was brought to my feet by a rapping at the window. Surprise! It was Glyn the District officer, carrying a bottle of "Johnny Walkers" whiskey, and as he and I were the only white men for at least 200 miles, he had decided that we should drink to Maloney that night and all the "silly buggers" who had ever set foot in this part of the globe called the "White mans grave". (Charming!)

During my travels around the area I was invited to see what was known as Fulani beatings. The young men of the Fulani tribe in a village, to pass into manhood, must walk in single file through a double line of their elders who, beat them with thin willow like branches. Crying out brought disqualification and shame I saw only one boy out of a dozen come through it. Blood was everywhere, but maidens of the village, singing as they went, carried him off in triumph.

I never failed to be amazed at the seeming disregard for human suffering by the African. A case in point was the day I came home to find a truck parked at my door. It was from the rail junction at Gudi it carried a few sticks of furniture sent to me from Lagos. As I walked up I could see that the driver had picked up some paying passengers on the way, and these people sat around on the grass beside the truck. Among these was a very old woman and a young boy, (of about ten years old) his head resting on her knee as she stroked his head crooning as she did so.

On closer inspection, I was horrified to see his right foot swollen to immense size and covered in dried blood. My first thought was that the truck had run over it, but no! I was wrong, the truck driver told me "it was a snake bite!" Now everyone in that country knows that this injury is fatal if not attended to at once. A medical facility was just down the road in Keffi village and here he was, yawning as he checked the coolant level under the hood. I was almost speechless to say the least, but I gabbled at him to "stop every thing and take the boy for treatment *Now*! He insisted however on removing the last article from the back of his truck before doing so. I called at the surgery later to see how the boy was, and was told that he had died, but *could* have been saved with attention that was more prompt.

Strolling thro the village one day I met a Syrian guy, he and I had a couple of beers at his house and we talked about many things, including the fact that he was running guns across the desert in the second world war to anyone who needed them. I mentioned that I was concerned about snakes getting into my house, and he assured me that "if you have cat, you no get snake". Indoors he was never bothered with snakes he said "because I got cat " it wasn't long before I also "had cat".

I would mention here that from time to time I called in the "Maigardi", (a local snake catcher,) he always caught a few snakes but more snakes would show up, it was quite a problem. After a while on a visit to Kaduna I responded to a note that was posted on the notice board by a member at the European club, "good home wanted for a Siamese kitten". I went around to the address at about teatime on a Sunday to meet this English family at their home.

I remember how the Lady of the house looked me up and down wondering, I imagine if I'd be suitable company for a Siamese Kitten and said she was concerned that as my wife would not be joining me for a week or so (actually she was due in eight weeks*) "Oh deceit thy name is man"* I thought I may not be able to cope. I began to wonder what exactly I let myself in for. His mother's name was "Celestine", his Grandmama, "Dusky Pearl of Singalore (I felt so inadequate) his father's name was unknown.

She regaled me of the habits of Siamese cats and what I should expect of him, (and what he would expect of me!) I began to wonder at the time, "who's going to be in charge?" She also informed me that these creatures had, as she put it, a daft half hour every day this means racing around the house, climbing onto or into everything in sight. Somewhat confused and carrying my new little friend I went down the path from the front door to the car clutching a list of instructions and a box of cat food, wondering if I could withstand the onslaught.

And so back to Keffi! I spent much time in the evenings trying to have this little guy respond to an exotic name, but the only one he liked was "Tommy". Anyway, I made his *official* name "Sarkin Kemwa" (King of Cats). The best laid plans of mice and men etc. He was to change my life forever, as I have not been without a Siamese cat since that time. As a matter of fact as I sit here typing this story so many years later I'm aware of two little Siamese kittens scuffling around my feet. I really must stop reading notice boards.

On my return to Keffi I was walking through the village one day looking to buy an extra dinner plate or two, when I saw to my total amazement a small English caravan parked outside a store I knocked on the door and it was answered by an English man: heavy set, gray beard, very distinguished looking. Within minutes, we were sitting in his caravan having beer served to us by his delightful Partner Margaret, an African lady. His name was Bob and he worked for the Posts and Telegraph Company, having a Roving Commission in the Northern Region he traveled around running overhead cables and lines where ever they were needed. He would employ local labour, do the job and then move on. He told me he had an aversion to busy towns, "too much gossiping and Politics" said Bob. He was happy just having his cheque sent to him each month.

74

One day Bob was to take Margaret to "Kaduna" so that she could take the train to her hometown to see her family, and I was invited along on the trip, we used Bob's small truck and took turns driving. Hot sticky and dusty, but we were used to it and made good time on the road. To pass the time we sang songs, it sounded strange to hear Margaret singing "Blaydon Races" but then I wonder what she thought of my rendering of an African Song, I guess I'll never know.

At times, the college would shut down for a long weekend holiday and the teachers that I knew went off to Kaduna or Jos for a break. At times like these living alone as I was, tends to send a man "Bush" so just to keep my sanity, I'd sometimes, sit on the veranda in the evenings, (with my recorder playing the songs I mentioned earlier) dressed in a suit and tie to have a drink, followed by Dinner, white table cloth, the lot! Hassan must have thought me a little crazy (perhaps I was). Looking back on my behavior I realize now that it must have been a few things that brought this on. Firstly, I missed the bustle of the city, (any city!) I missed the company of people I knew, the frustration of being 700 miles from the coast, just living for the weekly letter from Sheila and working in the heat for seven days every week to complete the job. (Phew! I feel better now).

A young Italian lad named Haraldo, about my age was in charge of the building project at the college and when work finished at Saturday lunch time we'd take turns at putting on a meal at our respective houses. Chicken Chop and beer at my place (Chop is "pidgin for food throughout West Africa) or Salami and Cheese, and Wine at his. I recall the time we caught a duika (Small deer) the Idea being that we'd fatten it up for Christmas, but one look at the Steward boy sharpening his knife, and we let him go. (The duika that is) Those big trusting eyes did it I guess.

The teachers and I, together with Glyn, converted an old Bush House into a small, informal Club. We named it "Maloney's Club" after the British District Officer murdered in the 1800's. As previously mentioned, we even had a Death Mask of Maloney hung on the wall.

On Saturday lunchtime whilst in the club quaffing a jar or two, the subject of Beards came up. I was told by one of the College teachers that he believed I could *not* grow a beard that would pass muster so to speak and to cut

a long Story short, I believed I could, so I bet beers all around that in six weeks, I could produce a "full set". I was then required to write a request to Glyn to "discontinue shaving". A "Jim's Beard" Night was arranged for six weeks hence in order to Judge the "Growth" in question. On the day concerned I found out that my "friends" had given the local barber five shillings to come to Maloney's Club at nine o'clock to shave off my beard, by force if necessary. Not wishing to comply I paid a visit to the barbers house in Keffi and gave him *ten* shillings to "forget all about it".

I went to the club that night and watched with some amusement the concern on the faces around me as the clock showed the time to be well after Nine o'clock. Furtive glances out of the window and some whispering followed, but soon it was apparent that I'd won, hands down, or perhaps I should say Chin down. There was much wailing and gnashing of teeth as I carried the Loot away. To reach my Gida I had to walk through very tall Elephant grass and although my little house was not too far away and lumbered as I was carrying a case of beer, wearing shorts, open toed sandals and short socks I was very lucky that I did not tread on any snakes or scorpions in the darkness. As a footnote let me tell you that as I sit here writing, that same Beard is turning a little gray but after all, it has been over 40 years.

The project was finished ahead of schedule and I prepared to return to the coast, Hassan asked to come with me but I told him it was not a good Idea as he was not so young anymore, The upshot being that, Emanuel, Hassan, myself and little Tommy piled into the car and went South.

In his time with me, Hassan told me many tales of the area, one, when he was a little boy in Keffi. The chief of a village not too far away sent horsemen to kill Maloney the District officer who, at the time was having dinner with the Chief of Keffi at his house. He was called outside the house by some ruse and was killed by an arrow then, beheading him they cast his head down a well. They were ordered to do this because Maloney had read him the riot act over slaving. As a little boy Hassan saw him buried by the villagers at the top of what is now called "Maloney's hill". I can see it now, this wizened old man talking to me, his bright eyes sparkling as he remembered all he had seen.

On my arrival at the Company office in Lagos for a debriefing with Bert, I was informed that I was invited to a Company party that very night. I accepted of course, besides I wanted to meet the other staff members and their wives. On my arrival at the party, I was greeted warmly, but noticed that some were scrutinizing me, I'd forgotten that a beard was almost unheard of at that time, except perhaps in the Navy. Some one told me in a loud voice what one of the wives was heard to say as I had walked in the door. "He looks like a cross between Abraham Lincoln and little Jesus" She was embarrassed at this, disclosure, but I told her I took it as a compliment, and said that I might have the wisdom of one, but no where near the Goodness of the other. She laughed.

Chaotic, is the word I'd use to describe Lagos at that time. I had forgotten that the celebrations for Nigeria's Independence were to be quite soon and everyone was in festive mood, with bunting in the streets, and new construction projects everywhere. It was a sight to see. Bert, who was just off to England on business, promptly loaded me down with projects all over Lagos, The Bristol Hotel, the new Tinibu Square fountain, the School for the blind, the School for those of impaired hearing and a few more besides. The Bristol Hotel was my main concern, and usually my first call each morning, although I quite often had a site meeting beforehand elsewhere.

It was when I arrived at the "Bristol" that the fun usually began. A fight between some guys on the fourth floor, some equipment stolen from the site store, or a man hiding his wife and kids in the basement, not to mention a visitor demanding arrears on house rent be paid up by a "palaver". Streets ahead would be my guess. It makes me wonder where West Africa would be today without the curse of congestion in the street traffic, wholesale piracy at the docks and on ships hove to offshore. Corruption increased at least hundredfold, electricity and water being shut off several times every day and massive unemployment I like to think that oil exports would be the answer, only time will tell!

Sheila arrived within a week of my trip down from the North. When she was at London Airport, Bert, who was on his way back to Lagos, had her paged at the information desk, introduced himself and they traveled back together to Nigeria. I had a Company flat in "Yaba" just outside Lagos on the mainland, where we set up house. As we arrived there, Sheila went straight to the Refrigerator, I heard a shriek as she saw the contents, I couldn't tell what the fuss was about as I'd just finished stocking up for the week, tinned stew, some beans and a six pack of Beer. Still, like the man said, "There's no pleasing everyone."

Within a week Sheila had turned the flat into a comfortable home for us to live in, and some home-cooked meals. Sheila really liked old Hassan as I did, but he didn't care for the city folk and the general bustle all around, and so it was that after a couple of months I took him to the Railway station and said goodbye, I know that I'll never forget him.

This period in my life was the busiest I've ever been, bar none. Out on the road by seven am, quite often calling into a project site meeting on the way. It was not unknown for me to be out on a site at 10 or 11 o'clock at night, or taking work home with me. It sounds crazy but I loved it.

I myself didn't have much luck when seeking help from any artisans outside of the Company, I remember that in Lagos I woke up one morning with a resounding toothache and not caring for severe pain I went in search of a dentist but without any success and was advised by someone to go the local hospital. I was introduced to the dental department and sat in the chair and as I expected, the tooth was to be extracted(ripped out of my head would have been a better description). But I was in no position to argue. I have a vague recollection that the "dentist" never washed his hands at any point, did not wear a white coat and I could see that the whole room was in need of a good scrub out.

This guy had never heard the word hygiene, but there I was being wrestled almost onto the floor I do believe that I screamed during the fracas. How I drove home, I'll never know, but I did, and collapsed into bed. It was the next day before I dared to look in the mirror at my gums. I was horrified to see that the place where the tooth used to be, resembled a miniature cesspool emitting an appalling odor. I think I was obliged to cling to my sanity right there where I stood. The following day the Company Doctor, upon seeing the ravaged gum was appalled and started me on a series of injections to draw out the filth and I might add, to restore my ragged Ego.

When I was in need of a haircut I'd head for the Kingsway store in the city centre, they had a large Barber shop on the first floor. It was here that one day I sat down on one of the four chairs and as the man worked away on my hair I began to sense that he was speaking to one of the other barber's in his own language next to him, apparently about me, He said he was "Pleased to see me" and asked me how my work was going. I didn't recall having met him before! It was then that he explained that he'd seen me at the week end at the Circus which was in town as the "star Rider" in the wall of death I was obliged to set him straight but as I left the store, I could tell by the grins on their faces that they certainly did not believe me and promised not to tell anyone about "my visit to the store"(or the Circus) I've heard it said many times that most everyone has a "Double" somewhere in the world and it seemed that I was no exception.

Sometime later in Ghana while working in an unused Emergency Operating theatre, of the new Korle Bu Hospital a nurse walked in carrying in her arms, a young injured boy. She gasped out; "Are you taking this one doctor?" I told her I was most certainly *not* the person she needed. And I quickly turned to go, as she looked at me in disbelief. After this, I looked in my wallet to make sure that I was in fact the person that I'd always believed that I was. It was my hope that whoever this character was, he would most certainly *" have to go"*, there isn't room in this town for the two of us.

By, the way, Kingsway was an amazing outlet, offering a wide range of Goods and Services, from Haircuts to Hatpins, Truck Tires to Telescopes. A veritable "Oasis" in the Desert. It was for this reason, that twenty-plus years later, I named my Corporate Video Media business "Kingsway Productions". The inference to Royalty ("King"-British origins) did not hurt either, and I managed to avoid the redundant nomenclatures of my Competition, i.e. "_____ Video Productions", et al, I believe that the "seriousness" of the name has worked during (my) Kingsway's 25 year existence . . . and with the advent of the Internet and other Media Distribution methods, the name has not pigeonholed the firm as just a "Video" Production Company. Over the years I've had many businesses of my own, from "Astral Appliances" to "Amway" , but Kingsway was really my forte.

Among our friends there in Accra were Jack and Pat Dawson, Jack was my immediate Boss, Bert Bampton (was head Honcho) and his wife Pam, Eileen and Billy Shields, a couple from Belfast, Billy was doing similar work to me. Pat, Eileen, Pam and Sheila became good friends I'm glad to say. Jack Dawson hailed from South Shields near Newcastle so we had something in common. There were other friends, Heaven knows, but the mists of time tend to dim ones memory, I'm afraid.

Very special among our friends was a couple from Scotland, Bob and Joyce Wilkie. I met Bob in the City, quite by accident. I took a friend's Phonograph (Record Player) in to be repaired as a favor. I was told that the gentleman recommended to me had gone back home, and that I should see the new Manager, a Mr. Robert Wilkie. He accepted the electronic device, promising prompt repair, and we had a chat over a beer. Later, Bob and Joyce were to have a profound effect on our lives forever. Robert Wilkie is one of most intelligent, interesting persons I've ever met, as is his

wife. Joyce is a beautiful and classy lady (I know Sheila will not take offense, as she also holds them both in high regard). Bob was, and still is, into all sorts of interests, from Archery to Real Estate. He shares my love of filmmaking to this very day. We spent every weekend together, alternating homes. Sundays quite often saw us all at the beach, and in so doing, we got nicely fried by the sun.

We acquired a puppy, and called him "Jerry". Paired with our Siamese cat named Tommy, we now had "Tom and Jerry" in our midst. Bob and Joyce moved to "Ibadan" after a while and we took turns visiting each other's houses on weekends a journey of about ninety miles, (but felt like 200 on that road) We both had 8 mm Cine Cameras by this time. The world waited with baited breath to see our movies (or so I'm told). One Sunday While on a trip to Lagos, Bob and I went out to shoot some film Of the City and decided that we would use the roof of the Bristol Hotel (a project I was involved with) to get this footage. After a while Bob climbed onto a Fan Housing to get a better view of things, a loud crash made me turn around only to see that Bobs camera had fallen onto the roof and lay there in pieces. Bob uttered some " words" which I will not repeat here, as he recovered it, but the day was spoiled so we went back to the house.

By Easter 1960 Sheila and I were at loose ends , so we went on a trip up north to Bida, a town well known for its brassware industry. We drove all day, and got as far as Jebba to stay the night. In the dining room after dinner we were enjoying cheese and crackers when I saw a Rhino beetle fly into the room, these creatures are about the size of a walnut with a large proboscis hence their name) Sheila underwent her insect baptism of fire so to

speak, as the invader bounced off a wall and fell into a newspaper she was reading. The meal was not exactly spoiled but we skipped dessert anyway. During the night, a huge storm came with very heavy rain, and the roof being thatched, literally thousands of bugs of every description were shaken into the room (Exit Jim and Sheila!) We reached Bida by lunchtime the next day and were in time to see some of the brass work being done. These craftsmen worked at their trade usually under the blazing heat of the sun. Using the most crude of hand tools, they fashioned brass work that is famous around the world. We made a purchase or two, and then walked into the town to watch a parade of Fulani horsemen in full regalia strutting their stuff. .Quite impressive.

We had Tea at the local rest house and later that night enjoyed a good dinner and stayed the night there. We were lucky that particular time as when Northern politicians are visiting a town they often take over the rest house, and we could well have been turned out, I guess there wasn't too many of them there on that visit. The trip back to Lagos took longer than we thought, as owing to the recent storm a huge tree (it was eight feet in diameter) was lying across the road a few miles away. The first vehicle to reach there was driven by yours truly and soon there was a long line of cars and trucks behind us, the drivers all yelling the odds as to how this should be handled (as though it was all my fault). In cases like this, the nearest village chief was responsible for seeing to it that the road was cleared.

In this instance, a village was close at hand and soon the chief himself came along to see the hold up. He first spoke to me (can't imagine why) telling me how he did not have enough men available, how his wife was very sick, and his many children needed him at home, plus he was *short of funds.* Suddenly I strongly wished that I were at the back of the queue instead of the front. The conversation went back and forth for an hour or so until there were forty vehicles or more behind us. Of course, I knew he would be paid for his trouble by the local Road Authority; he was just trying on the old African game of "getting a bit on top". It was only when I promised to put a word in for him at Head Office, that he relented.   Soon I saw a swarm of people climbing over the tree sawing sections off and hauling them to the roadside. It was thus, that we were allowed to proceed on our way.

About half way through this tour, the Company moved us to Adele Road in Apapa, a suburb of Lagos. In the apartment above lived Eileen and Billy Shields, a Belfast couple, we often attended the same parties around town (a popular pastime out there) where as the party progressed Eileen would invariably give us her rendering of "I'll take you home again Kathleen" very enjoyable. Billy was a two fisted drinking man and when his glass became empty, would declare "Jaysus this is a terrible dry house so it is", and when you brought a drink to him he would usually say "may your giving hand never fail you".

It was around this time that Sheila told me that she was pregnant. We were delighted, and began planning for the event, which would take place while we were on leave in England. At this point, we sent Tommy back to the UK on a KLM airplane to be quarantined for six months at some kennels in Bedfordshire after which he was to go to live with Uncle Son and Auntie Sis who told us later he really enjoyed his life there. A note here that when Tommy reached England and his carrier basket was opened, he was unable to stand. The flight he was on was delayed and he was over twenty-four hours inside his container on the plane. He was rubbed down and massaged then put in his living quarters until we picked him up. So much for KLM; "the animal lovers".

September 1960 Visitors came from all over the world to help celebrate Independence with Nigeria on the 1st of October. It was a very exciting time but I for one was glad when the noise died down and we could get back to a less frantic routine. When leave did come along, we booked passage on an "Elder Dempster" Mail Boat the **"Accra"** with a menu in the dining room that I for one will never forget. To give an Idea of the variety of food available even at breakfast, there were fourteen different kinds of Marmalade to choose from. I know I tried them all. This from a company that has been serving the West African coast since the first white man went there over a hundred and fifty years ago. Earlier I spoke about the impact that pidgin English has had on West Africa as a whole, although the educated African always decries its use today. However, it's the same pidgin that the well-heeled African uses on those less fortunate. As a means of communication, it was a Godsend to me. I would go as far as to say that without it, I'd still be there trying to get things done if it wasn't for Pidjin English. Further, I will note that a certain Religious order took it upon itself to produce the holy Bible in pidjin. *Quote* Noah "makee go fetch plenty beef dere for Ark. ....Big Ark *like Elder Dempster*".

Activities on board were many and varied if one wished to take part, and we did. I could be seen lurking on deck clutching my 8mm camera most of the time pointing it at everything and anybody in order to catch scenes for posterity. Activities   varied, from Bingo to Shuffle Board, swimming to horse racing, from Movies to treasure hunts, 14 Days of luxury and over half of it in the Tropics. A few hours in "Las Palmas" did us no harm either. The fancy dress ball was a great success presided over by the ship's commander; Captain Lightbody, as Emperor

Nero, attended by a friend of ours, a "Roman soldier" carrying a spear. Ladies of a Harem were to be seen along with "George Formby" and so many others. I myself, in Naval uniform was tagged as *"Captain Slightbody"*. Since that voyage we have also made the trip on the "Apapa" and the "Auriol", each one a memorable occasion.

On our arrival at Liverpool, heavily clad for the winter weather, we took the Boat train to London then a train to Hitchin and a Taxi to Walkern. Son and Sis made us welcome of course, and I was glad to see my little Ford Popular again, we used it to tour around Hitchin and Luton, and we paid a visit to see Glen and Joyce and enjoyed some Christmas shopping with them one afternoon in "Hemel Hempstead" but we stayed with the folks at Walkern.

Sheila went to the Herts and Beds Hospital to have the Baby, it was a Boy, and we called him Andrew, Much excitement. Next we took a plane to Dundee in Scotland, (Sheila had checked with the Doctor who said it would be OK to take the baby) to see Bob and Joyce Wilkie's folks, they made us very welcome, and took us all over the town to see their relatives. We would have lots to tell Bob and Joyce on our return. As I had my trusty 8mm Camera with me, I took footage of the Wilkie family members going about their business then went into town to get pictures of the stores all lit up for the Christmas season and of course the street decorations. I'm told that Bob and Joyce still have that little movie.

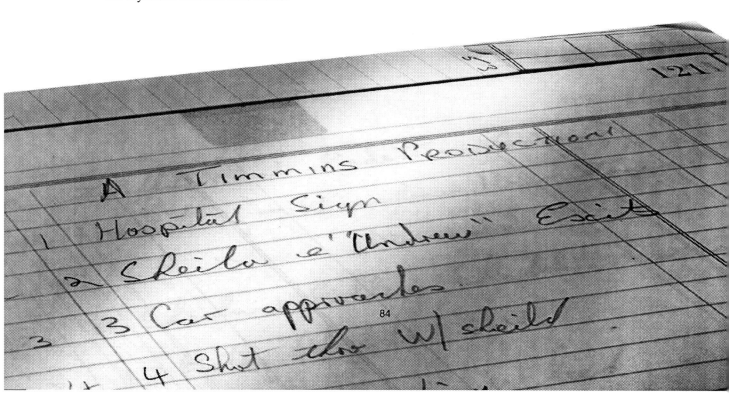

On our return to Hitchin we stayed at Sheila's Dad's for a weekend, it snowed overnight and left a good twelve inches, of the stuff everywhere. Deliveries in town were stopped for a day or so, my car sat outside looking rather silly with snow piled high on the roof, like a ridiculous hat. Sheila and I went to town, shopping and I took my cine camera in order to capture some of the snow scenes, it was all rather a giggle. A trip up North to Newcastle was on the agenda of course and we spent some time visiting Bobby and Agnes, then Sheila and young Peter, at their home, they made us very welcome. It was soon time to head south. On our way we took Peter to his school, I walked with him to the school door to say goodbye and as his eyes filled with tears, I tried to assure him that soon we'd be back.   I watched him walk away, his small shoulders drooping, I was aware of a lump in my throat that seemed to persist for some time.

My next assignment was to be "Ghana", so off we went, this time the three of us in a Bristol Brittania Turbo Prop Aircraft from London Airport. On our arrival in Accra, the Capitol, we were given a house outside of town in a place called "Manprobi." My work was to be on "Korle Bu" hospital, a huge project, about two miles from the house, it was said to be the largest of it's kind in all of Africa. Two other electrical Supervisors were already busy there, one, Les, a London man, was on the Surgical Block, and George from Manchester, the Maternity Block, Myself, I was to be concerned with the new children's section which was only then having the foundations completed Plus the new OPD which was being built adjacent to the original hospital.

About this time I got a letter from Pat and Jack telling us that Jerry our dog was being shipped to Accra airport and I was told of the time and date. On the day I went to pick him up, the clerk at the desk told me I must pay five pounds *"further"* tax. I knew that this "Tax" was also known as "Extortion". I knew for a fact that all legal taxes, fees, and expenses had already been paid in-full. I therefore refused to pony up this sudden "extra tax", and I informed him that I would relate this incident to higher authorities. It was at this point that he told me that "I should hasten to go and do that, and return quickly, as one never knows what a dog might find on the floor, eat it, and so poison himself". It seemed that he'd covered all bases. I realized that in Africa this was known as "taking care of business" so of course I handed five pounds "Dash" to the brave policeman. But I saved my dog.

It was a change from the frenetic pace in Nigeria, and just one site to be concerned with, after a few weeks Jack Dawson showed up and was my boss, as well as Bert Bampton (who was contracts manager on site), Much to my delight, Emanuel traveled all the way from Eastern Nigeria to work at Korle Bu. After some months, we moved house again, this time into, a compound in the town centre. As was usual in West Africa we employed a night watchman for security. This not withstanding one night we had a visit from a burglar or "Tief Man" to use the vernacular, later the watchman swore he was not asleep but saw "nothing" anyway. Jerry's barking in the living room woke us up just in time for the intruder's exit out of the bedroom window, but he only got some small change for his trouble.

The thing that bothered me was the fact that he came into our bedroom, went through my pants pockets and Sheila's purse before Jerry convinced him to leave. All this while we were lying there asleep. I understand that a local Ju Ju man probably sold him a piece of pink lint with a magic spell on it, or something similar that, if clutched in his hand he would be invisible to the occupant should he wake up. (Maybe it's true because I didn't see him).

I met a number of expatriates who were to my mind eccentric, during my stay on the West Coast. One was the English construction boss on a very large block of flats being built near the coast when I was in Lagos. I knew him as Claude, and I felt that we got on quite well. I was allowed according to "the book" to have a full day for my crew to install the various electrical conduits in each bay of the building floor after he had the steel rebar completed, before his people could be allowed to pour concrete in a given section. I can only guess that he harboured some sort of grudge against me (maybe it was something I'd said), as he brought his crew in on the Sunday and did just that! The Architect was furious, and made him cut grooves cut all over the concrete floors to accommodate my conduits.

Funnily enough, down the road, he and I became good friends. Many years later I was to learn that during the second world war, his skills at opening locked safes caused the government

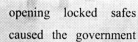

to call him back from a period of "Incarceration" to work for his Majesty's pleasure and "do some work behind enemy lines." There was even a film made of his escapades.

The Ambassador Hotel

A gentleman I knew only as Willie during my time in Lagos was always in the bar at the club, standing there holding forth on his favourite subject- himself. He claimed that he did not like to drink "its just my hobby, so fill yer boots" and on and on and on . . . ad-infinitum. Very boring.

Korle Bu OPD

I well remember a guy at Port Harcourt, Nigeria doing similar work to mine, for a company called Nigerlec. He asked me to dinner one night at his house, introduced me to his wife then we sat down for a drink. As my gaze wandered around I saw a huge photograph above a mantelshelf of a naked lady reclining full length it was six feet long by twelve inches wide, bad taste I thought, even then. It was I thought, put there to impress any, and all visitors. After dinner while his wife was in another room I ventured to ask him who it was, his answer was oh that? It's my wife! Oh well I thought, ask a silly question etc. But I digress, now back to Accra Ghana.

As I had a 8mm camera I joined a small cine group who were interested in the same thing, it was made up of about six English guys and their wives, meeting at different homes once a week. I learned a lot as we went along; we even made a movie after a while called "It's Only Money" (Starring guess who?) I would add that this Title was my idea and was in existence twelve months before the Hollywood Production of that name. (Fame at last). We met and became friends with a guy called Len and his wife Marion in this group, he was seconded out to the Ghanaian Air force from the RAF, we spent a lot of time together during our stay.

Little Andrew seemed to thrive in Africa, he toddled around in which ever Company house we might be living in, usually accompanied by "Jerry" who, lets face it, always hoped that Andrew would drop a few crumbs from some "Goody" Mam had given him. Jerry was a great companion to me, and was very protective of Andrew- growling at any stranger who approached his young charge. He is sorely missed.

Sheila and other Company wives visited each other of course, and had occasional meetings for coffee, brought any children they had to play, swap news etc. On these days the men folk would come there from work, have a beer and take their family home.

Half a dozen of us went for a picnic one Sunday to "Aburi" a place up in the hills. We stopped by a small lake to unpack, just then, young Andrew shouted "crocodile!" and ran towards what I thought had been a log at the lake side, I dived after Andrew to stop him, and watched as this ugly great creature slid into the lake. I could have used something stronger than Tea *that day*. On a later visit to this place I was carrying Andrew in my arms as I ran down a small pronomotory which ran down into the lake, almost to the edge I skidded to a halt as I saw, not six feet away the unmistakable snout of a huge crocodile protruding above the surface. Turning around I ran up the slope and if I had not remembered that we had a car with us I am sure I would have ran all the way home, (So much for the Great White Hunter!)

Bob and Joyce came to visit us on their way home to Scotland on leave, and told us they intended to Emigrate to Canada after visiting the folks. Sheila and I were hoping to Emigrate to New Zealand and were writing letters to that effect, Bob and Joyce seemed to think we ought to follow on to Canada after our tour was up, but the notion of all that snow, Ugh. Any way we said we'd keep in touch.

I did two tours in Ghana and the whole time we were there the President, Kwame Nkrumah went in fear for his life, there was always a "State of Emergency" and a curfew in effect. Roadblocks on the way to work, house searches and Palaver everywhere. The Politics in town varied from childish to the appalling, like the time an English bank managers wife bought a dress at a store and was accosted in the street by an African woman who said that she saw it in the store first and it was rightly hers. This woman was, it turned out, a friend of the Chief of Police. This being so, the police went to the Bank manager's house and demanded satisfaction, however he was not to be bullied and so supported his wife on her purchase.

The result was that they were ordered onto a plane for UK that same evening. Incidents like this were happening all over we were told. The saddest aspect to all of this, was the empty stores *everywhere*, large stores, with their roots in many European countries, were bereft of most every thing . . . no clothes or overseas newspapers, no clothes pegs, paint, nor even tires for your car. One day I was in the local market place, when a friend of mine sidled up to me, and after looking around furtively whispered in my ear telling me where Corn Flakes cereal could be had. Without looking up, I raced to my car and sped off like a maniac. Once in the store, I stood panting for breath gazing around at nothing else but empty shelves (and this establishment was the size of a large American "Safeway's" grocery store). Undaunted, I went over to where corn flakes *should* be but to no avail. Frantic by now, I found an assistant, gasping out my request saying that I had come from Kumasi (100miles away) after hearing that he alone had the key to the Corn flake cupboard in Accra.

After making sure that no one had overheard, he disappeared like a wraith into the storage area reappearing clutching a brown paper package for me in one hand. The other one was outstretched, palm up, however "I had *no change with me"*, so shaking his hand I told him that I thought he was "doing a fine job." Outside the store, more palaver, a local urchin told me that he couldn't help but notice that one of the tires on my car was almost bald, and that if I would care to step down the alley he could show me a tire for a very good price. I started the car and left a cloud of dust behind. The black market was booming all around and to give an Idea how we got around some of the shortages you must hearken to the following tale. Frank Vocking, our company Contracts Manager, was not unaware of our plight concerning "necessary," Items, and enquired of all company personnel as to what they might be in need of. One of the things *we* were desirous of was cheese, among many other things. Frank with an empty suitcase in hand, flew to Lagos, Nigeria to do a little shopping. On his return, going through customs, his "luggage" was left alone in exchange for a small "consideration."

That evening when I came home from work, I found Sheila in a high state of excitement. Frank had stopped by and left some goodies including some English Cheddar cheese. Slices were cut that night no thicker than razor blades and enjoyed immensely. The meal reminded me of an oasis in the desert such was the relish with which we ate. All of this not withstanding, Leader Kwame Nkrumah, instigator of this situation, was later "de-throned", and died in exile.

For our first Leave from Ghana we had ordered a Motor home, a "Commer Highwayman". We picked it up at "Wilsons", a dealer in Brixton. First stop; a Grocery store to stock up. We toured England Scotland and Wales, then France and Spain, quite a trip. Moreover, the vehicle drove like a dream.

It has been said more than once that "It's a small World" and this was amply demonstrated to me when we chanced to go to the town of "Chester" on this particular trip. We had parked in a campground, and pushing Andrew in a stroller, we wandered around the town taking in the sights. We stopped on a street corner and were bemoaning the fact that we were unable to find a Launderette in the town. Just then, a familiar voice addressed me from behind! "Why not come home with me and have dinner? And do your washing there?" I turned around and, of all people; it was Tony Blair, late of Keffi! After many incredulous remarks, hand shaking etc. we did as Tony asked, and so he brought us to his home, where Selma was equally surprised, we had a very pleasant visit, and Selma gave us the use of the laundry room.

Today, as I sit here, having spent six years on the West African Coast, and met hundreds of European people who worked long hours in their numerous Trades and professions, building an infrastructure the African People could be proud of, I sometime wonder if it has all been for nothing. Since leaving there, I've learned that civil war, famine, anarchy and insurrection is common. Lawlessness seems to prevail, where once stood thriving communities; I see no peace ahead for this poor benighted Continent.

All of this notwithstanding, when the time came to leave Africa for good, we were very sad. Looking back, since we left, both African countries that we lived in have had more than their share of problems. I do hope that there are better times to come. I still like to think that perhaps in some small way I made a contribution to their future. I have read quite a few books about the exploits (good and bad) of District Officers, Forestry Officials, and UK Construction and Service personnel. These amazing men and women helped build the nations of the African continent for the eventual self-governance by it's native people. Overall, I believe that the climate and the conditions took a toll on all concerned during the last two hundred years. I hereby salute them all, no matter where they may be. In the years that followed, I did write to Emanuel Okeke, but there has been no response. There is a chance that he did not survive the civil War that occurred after we left. I do hope that I am wrong.

By this time, Bob and Joyce had left Canada and moved to Santa Clara, California in the U.S.A. We'd been swapping letters and tapes all this time and they encouraged us to consider emigrating to California. In case dear reader, you are wondering whether we did or not, I'm writing this "Tome" in my Santa Clara living room, 50miles due South of San Francisco, having lived here for almost forty years.

From Ghana, we went to England to say our goodbyes and have a short holiday, We booked passage with Elder Dempster on the "Auriol " It was on this final trip from Africa that we ran into a force eleven gale which we were told qualified it as a Hurricane. (And on that point, I had no argument, believe me) Monstrous waves battered the ship and the windows on the bridge shattered as passengers and crew cowered before the onslaught. It started during the night as we sailed in the South Atlantic, and by mid morning it became so violent that the Captain had the ship "Heave To". It was then that passengers were told that Liverpool was so busy that she could not take personal radio messages. It was a very sobering experience and I for one became very much aware of my vulnerability in the scheme of things.

Meals in the dining room for those who felt able to eat were to say the least, tricky. Sitting as I was, soup spoon in hand waiting for the bulkhead to return to perpendicular so I could imbibe a little soup. I witnessed one quite large lady, who had given up any thoughts of eating and carrying two valises of what appeared to be personal items she stood up. It was at this at this point that the forces of nature took a hand and the ship began a wicked roll to port. Causing the lady in question to begin running down the oblique sloping deck to the exit. It was fortuitous that the burly chief steward was on hand and he flung out his two arms and saved her from injury.

Before darkness fell, the captain decided that we should make a run for it, and so it was that we docked at the "Pool" along with broken windows on the Bridge, heaps of broken crockery, together with some bruised egos. We spent a month saying our farewells to friends and family then toured a little, as a still small voice told me I must be insane to leave dear old England. Maybe I was but the spirit of adventure still burned brightly in both Sheila and me and so we took our leave and tried not to look back.

END OF THE BEGINNING

We embarked on the "Queen Elizabeth" at Southampton, bound for New York. We traveled tourist on this trip to conserve our resources, (save money too) *Joke*! She was of course absolutely Gigantic, beautifully appointed, with a romantic history. But stabilizers notwithstanding, she had a wicked roll in a particular sea. It's a moot point I suppose as in later years, when she was sold as scrap to a Company, she caught fire when moored off Hong Kong and capsized. A tragic end to a much loved ship.

I recall my first contact with anyone in America was that of an Irish porter who was handling our cases on the dockside, seeing the labels of our destination indicated California he asked why, I replied that we had friends there. Oh! He cried. Not for meself boyo! I have been here in America 18 years and I'm staying here at the waterside begob, ready to go back to the old sod if I need to. (Trying to encourage a newcomer like me I suppose)

From New York, we flew T.W.A. to San Francisco and were met by Bob and Joyce and we stayed with them a week or two, it was good to see them again. The Date: February 1965. They took us everywhere showing us the area they lived in, the Stores (huge! What selections! Electronics! The fresh food and Produce! . . and one could select what exact fruits and vegetables one wished to purchase!); a Hamburger Drive In, "Flea Markets" and "Garage Sales", the expansive Beaches and Hills, all connected via massive multi-lane freeways. They even introduced us to the Western Rodeo. Bob and Joyce would speak expansively of all the economic and living opportunities in this diverse, and exciting country. We took to America immediately, and over the years absorbed a Way Of Life that we have come to love dearly. Somewhat like the original British men and women who founded this nation, the Timmins' Clan adopted the United States as a new Home.

Automobiles are a necessity here. Our very first night we were taken to what was called a "Drive-In Movie", where we saw a brand new American comedy film (set in California) called "It's a Mad, Mad, Mad, Mad World". Great fun. We spent most of our weekends together with Bob and Joyce. Those were the Best Of Times.

I obtained a Driving License and took a Maintenance job at a General Motors plant where I stayed for twelve months. To be nearer to the job we moved a few miles up the freeway to Fremont, a small apartment. Sheila told me at this time that we were going to have another baby and this being so I realized that we would have to look for a house of our own. Because of my background in such work I just had to try a construction job, I found that to do so I would have to go through the local union, well I did so and spent a few months on different Commercial jobs around the area. It was very different to any other contract I'd been on.

It was whilst I was working at General Motors that we found a house we liked, three Bedrooms, two Bath rooms, and a two car garage. We bought some second hand Furniture, a Washing Machine . . . even a Lawn Mower (*another* "necessity" here in California). With only thirty Dollars left in the Bank after these purchases and the Mortgage Down Payment; we signed the Papers, and put our Key in the front door lock of our own Home...The property was ours.

Once I decided that working on Construction would not work out I took a job about seven miles from where we lived, at least it would be a steady paycheck. I found that at times, Electricians were detailed to go to the Body-Build –Shop to service the electric welding guns. Workers were stationed along side of the conveyers. Using the various guns suspended overhead at intervals, they "manhandled" these massive tools into various locations on the car body, performing the welds as the vehicle passed by, The thundering noise and flying sparks in this "Dantes Inferno" was not new to me as I had Worked at an Auto Plant in Luton England just after I was married.

However, I found some relief of my own making, So hearken to my tale. The cars had to pass on the conveyor over a concrete lined pit, this enabled the Welders to work on the lower section of each unit. It so happened that we had visitors one day, a group of about twenty High school youngsters guided by a security guard. I was at the time in the pit repairing a gun, my face being at floor level I was seen to be a self made grotesque sight, hair combed over my face, Back hunched, body somewhat twisted with face distorted carrying a belt full of tools, a young Lady, unable to bear the sight before her, leaned forward, crouched down and asked me in a pitying voice if I always had to work down there I gabbled a reply as she thrust a lollipop into my hands and ran back to her friends. It was my way of getting the word out I suppose. I sometimes wondered if it was reported in high places! Still it relieved the boredom.

By now the baby's arrival was close. One evening we settled down to watch television. A good movie was on; "*Man Without A Star*" starring Kirk Douglas, Partly into the broadcast, Sheila informed me that "This is the **time** . . . we have to go *now*". We sped off to Kaiser Hospital, and I left her in the able care of the Doctors and Nurses, While she did all the hard work, I paced up and down the Waiting Room, as New Fathers are wont to do. Years later, with to the advent of VHS movies, I was able to see the ending to that great Western film,

The following morning I woke up to the phone ringing. It was Sheila and I was told that we had a little girl. Still in a daze, I went over there armed with my cine camera, and took pictures of our new little girl and her Mum. We watched little "Julie" grow as the years went by, and never failed to be amused and delighted at the way she sort of jiggled as she went around the house playing. So I nicknamed her "Jiggling Jules". Andrew adored her, and was very protective, We had a nice little family, even if I do say so myself.

There were quite a few English people among the skilled trades, at the Ford Plant. John Stenhouse, a machinist, (he was brought up in Brighton) became a friend of mine, and at one point he was on vacation at the same time that we were visiting England, around 1972 I believe.   He invited us to tea and to meet his family while we were on the South coast, a very enjoyable visit I might add. An English electrician who came from Cheshire in England came to work at the Ford plant and became my closest Buddy He arrived not long after I began working there. His name: Johnny Jones, he and I worked on various projects together in the plant as the years rolled by and of course Sheila and I became very close friends with John and his wife Marian.

Our favourite vacation as years went by was Disneyland, there was something there for young and old. We'd drive down in a big old Mercury station wagon, the usual Family trip ("are we there yet Dad?"), and singing, guessing games, cold drinks, 500 miles on Highway 5. Staying at a Motel, to my mind, is a thing to be avoided, but the kids thought it the best thing since sliced bread, ("Dad look we've got our own TV"). We all enjoyed Disneyland of course but, at the end of the day that Motel looked very attractive, and oh! my poor feet. Even so, there came a day when Julie refused to leave Disneyland until she met "Mickey Mouse". Poor Dad.

Eight years later Sheila told me we were going to have another addition to the family, I can't recall who was the most thrilled, and right away we set about organizing the Welcome for our new family member. We must have looked and sounded like a couple of teenagers at times. In due course Sheila presented us all with a little boy, we called him "Sean". As he grew we hovered over his every step forward he was very fortunate to have his "big" brother and sister there and each day I watched them hurry home from school to play with their new brother.

Julie and Andrew attended McCoy School in their early years and they tell me now that they enjoyed it. Andrew went on to "Wilson" Junior High and then to "Bellarmine Preparatory School". Julie did her High School years at "Santa Clara High". Andrew held various jobs before joining the Army, and Julie worked in the Banking Industry.

When the time came, Sean attended Haman grade school and I observed as the pressures of school began to get in the way of every thing else regarding Sean's life. It was because of this that we declared ourselves a "School at Home" and Sheila, with help from Andrew or me when it was needed, worked with him. We watched the lad leap ahead of his Peers. Sean graduated High School with high marks, gaining his California Diploma at age Sixteen. Looking back, I think the gravest disservice that I've done to my Children, is not "seeing the need" for all of them to be out of Public School.

I spent almost twenty years at the Ford Plant mostly on Swing shift and watched as they built many of Ford's finest models. For the final seven years, I became the Representative for the Skilled Trades people in the "United Auto Workers Union, It proved to be most interesting, and a privilege I'll never forget. It brought forth abilities that I did not even realize that I possessed.

In 1981-82, Andrew volunteered for service in the U.S. Army and spent four years during the height of the Cold War in Germany, troubleshooting Helicopter Electronic Weapons Systems. He says he learned a lot, and loved the European travel . . . but he is happy to be a civilian, and plot his own course now.

It was a blow to everyone in the plant when Ford announced that the Plant would close in six months time, the deadline being April 1983. It was six months of long faces in the plant, but then people began to plan and reshape their future, there was training available in many fields and it made for a smoother transition, but the closing tore apart many families. A good friend of mine, Joe, who worked in the plant, volunteered to do the Video work that the company needed and because I was interested, I was allowed to help at times. This led to me bringing in my own camera to shoot things that I wanted, even after the plant closed. After a while I started a Video business doing projects of various kinds for companies in the area including I might add Ford Motor Company as ten years later they converted the auto plant into a shopping mall and requested that the whole procedure be recorded to tape by Kingsway Productions.

It never fails to amaze me how time flies by, it seemed like only yesterday that little "Jiggling Jules" stood there in Disneyland stamping her foot, demanding to meet Mickey Mouse before she left for home, and now here she was, telling me that their was another man in her life besides me.

I met "Jamie" soon afterwards and knew that I could not wish for a finer young man for my Daughter. They were married in San Jose soon

afterwards, it was a happy day indeed, but also quite emotional, I remember, I seemed to be joking very hard as the Limousine took us to the Church.

1991. Julie and Jamie presented to the world a baby Boy, his Name: Daniel James, (James after me) We're Grand parents! I have read somewhere that Grand Parents always think that "their child" is Cuter than the ones in other families, Not true of course! *Nevertheless,*, guess what? Daniel most certainly was!

Early in 1991 Sheila and I went on our third Vacation to England, we visited our folks of course and then had some time to ourselves just enjoying the English Countryside. I have a regret in my life, like most people I guess, and that is that I've not been in one place long enough to really get to know my family,. My sister Margaret helped me come to terms with it on this trip, and to makeup for lost time. Margaret and Josie, her friend, welcomed me, put me up, and fed me delicious meals. Then took time off to run me around the area to explore the Old Home Town.. I have to add, that all of this was flavoured with many giggles together, including dancing on the grass with Josie at Seaton Sluice. Needless to say I've had offers from Hollywood so Josie, if you're interested... At one point Sheila and I went to Eastbourne, as she had family business to take care of. In the middle of all of this, I took a side trip to Brighton to see Pat and Jack Dawson   I had a small Camcorder with me and brought back home a record of our visit, which included Hitchin, Eastbourne, Newcastle of course, and Wigton To where I was evacuated in 1940. When we were up North, we visited our old favourite: Beamish "Open Air Museum" it must be seen to be believed, a huge area transformed into a scene of the early 1900's. On our return to the States, I edited the footage together to make a record of our trip and it turned out quite well.

A few months have passed and we learned that Sheila's Dad was very sick in Hospital, Sheila went back to UK to be with him, But he passed away after two weeks. It was only a short while ago that I was there with him, finally spending some time getting to know him.

At the time that Sheila was in England, I got a call from our dear friends Pat and Jack Dawson. They were over here in the States to take care of some family business in Oakland and would like to come over for a few hours; I was bowled over to say the least (it's been over 30 years). The pity is that Sheila was still in England. However, I picked them up at the Fremont BART. Station (our Rapid Transit System) just twelve miles up the Freeway and brought them here to our house then we spent the rest of the day reminiscing about West Africa, Boy! Did we ever.

As I write, it is Sean's seventeenth Birthday, and so if you will excuse me, I'll go and have some cake and ruminate as to where all the years have gone.

April 1992- Julie and Jamie called by today, bringing little Daniel of course, he's developing splendidly, was a Joy to be with, and is on the verge of crawling around. Julie told us today that she is again Pregnant, we're thrilled to bits for them, another Grandchild! Whoopee! This time a little girl; Carrie.

Well. Dear reader once again, years have passed and here it is 1993. It's been ten years since the Ford plant shut down, but Ford has returned to the scene and is now getting ready to build a large shopping mall on and around the skeleton of what used to be the assembly plant, and I've been asked to videotape it in it's entirety. Apparently, it is to be the fourth largest in California, the wreckers have already been at work and we're told that the project is to be completed by the fall of 1994.

Daniel
Kanu

In 1996, Julie and Jamie adopted a little boy from Sierra Leone and I'm pleased to say that Kanu is thriving along with Daniel and Carrie. The family grows apace! And Lo' in 1997 my son Sean presented us with a grand daughter named "Taylor", and in 1998 Julie brought forth another scrumptious Beautiful little girl named Molly. The Timmins family is blessed many times over.

Now, the 21st Century is upon us, and I have finally retired, to give myself some time to do some of the little audio, video, and writing projects I always wanted to finish, and perhaps lookup some old friends and extended family.

Taylor

Taylor is nine, has a penchant for Writing, Science, and Performance, and attends special schooling for the "intellectually gifted". She fairly bubbles with ideas and optimism, and seems to be the "leader" that her peers are naturally drawn to. The future appears to be wide open to her choosing. Whether the Calling is Science or the Arts, I wish only that she be happy.

Julie is very actively involved with her local Schools in many different ways. Her husband (my Son-In-Law), Jamie Mathews is the Hazardous Materials Code Enforcer for the City Of San Jose. He divides his "spare" time between Family, and Service as a member of the Santa Clara City Council. His family has been in the area for generations, thus he is keen to preserve History, maintain the Environment, develop this "Family Friendly" City, and expand Business. Its early days, but he currently leads next year's electoral race to become the next Mayor of Santa Clara.

Carrie   Jamie   Julie   Molly   Daniel   Kanu

Andrew has taken the helm of the family business **KINGSWAY.DYNAMIC.MEDIA** with a vengeance, and transformed it . . ,producing custom DVD, and Web programs for Corporations in Silicon Valley. Sean still lives in the Bay Area, and has joined his brother in this venture. The year 2006 marks the 25th Anniversary of KINGSWAY PRODUCTIONS. I'm so gratified to be able to bequeath this to my sons, although Andrew says "Dad, you've *always* given me *"The Business"*.

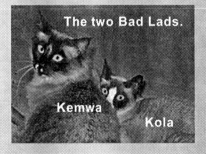

The two Bad Lads.
Kemwa   Kola

99

If Sheila and I thought when we got married that we were merely starting a little family, we've had to take another look. I really get a charge as I quietly observe the development of my Grandkids, and see how they handle various things whilst playing. Molly might share some secret Treasure she has found with me in whispered tones, Carrie will unveil her latest Art Project, as Taylor articulates some new words she's added to her vocabulary. Meanwhile, Daniel and Kanu are locked in Musical or Sports competition; All are "Grist for the Mill of Life", I guess. There goes Granddad waxing poetic again!. Despite Life's trials and tribulations, I have been blessed with a loving Wife, Children, and Grandchildren . . . my *own* Businesses, and a chance to see The World. I've had the opportunity to follow *my own Path*, and see the Light . . *As Big As The Sky* .

James Timmins, April 2006

Not Quite | FIN

Please contact the Author
with any serious enquiries:
jamestimmins@sbcglobal.net

Professional Dramatized Audio
Versions of this book, with
Narration, Music, and Sound
Effects, are also available.

Book Design and Layout by
KINGSWAY PRODUCTIONS TEL.408.881.2485
WWW.KINGSWAYPRODUCTIONS.COM

*This is not "**The End**"...*

*Nor is this "**The Beginning of The End**"...*

*It is, perhaps, "**The End of The Beginning**"*

Sir Winston Churchill

LaVergne, TN USA
21 September 2009
158543LV00001B/74/A